SIDETRACKS

SIDETRACKS

40 True Stories of Hunting and Fishing
on Paths Less Traveled

GARY OBERG, BME, PE
with TRINA HOLT, MSc

Rose City Press, Minnesota, USA

ISBN-13: 978-1-79039-220-9

BISAC CODES

BIO026000   BIOGRAPHY & AUTOBIOGRAPHY / Personal
                     Memoirs
SPO022000   SPORTS & RECREATION / Hunting
SPO014000   SPORTS & RECREATION / Fishing

Book Cover Design Art Director: Joan Holman

Website: www.mysidetracks.com

Gary Oberg
P.O. Box L
Dassel, Minnesota 55325

To Ginny, Dawn, and Troy

The woods are lovely, dark and deep,
but I have promises to keep,
and miles to go before I sleep,
and miles to go before I sleep.

— ROBERT FROST

ACKNOWLEDGMENTS

MANY THANKS TO TRINA HOLT for her help in bringing life to my stories by adding dialogue, details, and color. My gratitude to Tom Lutz for his help in structuring my stories into book form. Thanks to Tracey Finck for her sharp copy editing. Deb Koep, thanks for the cover photo. Appreciation to Joan Holman for the final production details.

I'd also like to share my gratitude and appreciation for my hunting buddies, especially Quintin Clark, who mentored me early on and taught me many fishing and hunting tricks. Finally, to my mother and dad for their prayers that still follow, even after their passing.

CONTENTS

FOREWORD

WHEN GARY FIRST APPROACHED ME about helping him put together a book of his fishing and hunting expeditions, I had a moment of hesitation. I'd been a vegetarian for more than 20 years and lived in cities for most of my adult life. Could I relate to an avid outdoorsman like Gary? That said, my husband got me interested in steak again, and I've been ocean sailing and boating for more than 20 years now. I grew up in the dense forests of the interior of British Columbia, Canada. I know all about how beautiful, and treacherous, the woods can be, and I know even more about the draw of the ocean and the rugged West Coast. My dad taught me to shoot gophers when I was about eight, and I rode my first horse when I was five. He took me fishing often, and sometimes we hunted rabbits, grouse, or ducks. I figured I could draw on these early-life experiences, so I accepted the challenge.

As it turned out, it was a delight. Gary emailed me story after story that had me laughing or hanging on to the edge of my seat. It was my job to polish his remarkable tales and turn them into a book. Although I tried to stay as authentic to his originals as I could, I did add some colour here and there in the form of dialogue or description. If you spot any inaccuracies, they will most likely be mine, not Gary's. I did my level-best to write it as I thought Gary would tell it, and he tried to keep me honest.

It's been a real trip going on this journey with him, and

I'm grateful for the opportunity. It was a fun challenge to step into his well-walked shoes. I've learned so much! Mostly, I am deeply honoured for the trust he's put in me.

Thank you, Gary.

So, without further adieu, I have a date with my husband on the rooftop of our very modern condo nestled into the very heart of our West Coast city, where he is barbequing us some steak and salmon. Who knows, maybe someday I'll take a side-track of my own and try eating moose.

Trina Holt
December 5, 2018

1 • SIDETRACKS

I'VE NEVER SEEN A BULL moose walk down Main Street at high noon during hunting season. The biggest moose, the finest deer, and the feistiest fish all have one thing in common: they keep off the beaten path. To find them, you have to take the sidetracks.

Sidetracks are full of rewards and prizes but only for those who are willing to face risks and endure some discomfort. I've found this to be true not only for fishing and hunting, but for life in general. If you're not living on the edge, you're taking up too much room.

I've tried to live this way and, for the most part, I can honestly say that for me, it's been the right way to go. I'm not saying it's all been sunsets and fish dinners—I've eaten more than my share of canned beans in the rain—but for all my failures, the best, most memorable parts of my life have come as a result of taking sidetracks.

Some people think that R&R means rest and relaxation, but to me, R&R means risks and rewards. When you walk the sidetracks, you're always thinking about how to mitigate risk. With fishing and hunting, I'm always aware of gun safety, weather patterns, loose rock, and all manner of nature's boobytraps. I've learned to be careful about what I eat and drink and try not to become some animal's lunch. Sometimes half the challenge is just getting to the destination: planes, trains, trucks, boats, horses, snowmobiles, and motorcycles all have their inherent challenges and dangers. And then there's the human factor. Just as in city-life, when you're in the wilderness, you must be mindful of other people. I wear blaze orange to *not* get shot, I try to follow the rules, I share and share alike, and generally try to keep the peace.

My rewards for taking all those risky sidetracks are immense and plenty. First, there isn't one single day when I've been in the wilds and haven't taken a moment just to appreciate God's great creation. Everywhere I look, I see beauty. Every breath I take is fresh. Every sound is pure. Those moments, on their own, are perfectly valid reasons to march straight into the deepest forest. Sometimes I go home empty handed. The game outplays me and the fish out-smart me. Fair enough. But usually, I get to fill my freezer with fish and game. Often, I get to spend time with other like-minded people and develop terrific friendships built on a foundation of laughter and shared interests. I almost always go home with a solid sense of accomplishment, and sometimes, when things go really right (or really wrong) I even gain a little wisdom. My beard is grey now, but I'm still young at heart. I can't ask for more than that.

My road has definitely been bumpy and less travelled, but now, after six decades of following sidetracks, I have a lifetime of stories to share. I'm rich with experience, friendships, family, and I have a deep faith in God and all His creation. What I *don't* have, are regrets.

● ● ● ●

Fishing and hunting areas around where I live.

2 • CHARLIE BUDD

MY GOOD FRIEND QUINT AND I had been hunting for a couple weeks, but so far, we didn't have a thing for all our efforts. However, we still had some time left in the season. Determined, we decided to try our luck at Sturgeon Landing, Saskatchewan, Canada, over the Thanksgiving weekend in late November 1968. It would give us a chance to hunt on snow, which is always a tremendous advantage when hunting moose.

Sturgeon Landing is an Indian settlement not far from the Saskatchewan-Manitoba border. It perches on the northeast corner of the very large Namew Lake and isn't exactly the easiest place to get to. A long paved highway eventually becomes a rugged logging road. Driving a four-door Ford car on that road was no mean feat. The wheel ruts were deep enough to bury a coyote. Few traveled that road, which was a good thing because if we ever did come across another vehicle, one of us would have inevitably ended up stuck. Fortunately, the remoteness of the area was nearly complete. It took us two hours to travel 20 miles on that road, hoping and praying that it was the *right* road, before we finally arrived at Sturgeon Landing.

Sturgeons, as locals fondly referred to it, had a population of 150 Indians, and Ken, the Caucasian. Ken was a blue-eyed, fair-haired, fast-talking guy. He stood about five-foot-ten and was lean. Ken had the complete village under his financial control—a fact that he boasted on.

"I own the general store, and I'm the outfitter, grocer, post master, and banker," Ken told us proudly. "Government checks come in on the postal-service plane on the third Wednesday of every month. I usually get to keep every one of 'em because I advance credit against them."

About the only thing he didn't control was the police, but the native people had that covered.

"A couple of years ago," Ken told us, "one Indian boy shot and killed another Indian boy. When the Canadian Mounties came and investigated, they asked a lot of questions but only got a lot of silence. After being stonewalled for a couple days, they gave it up and went back home."

I guess what happens in Sturgeons, stays in Sturgeons.

We arranged for a guide on this trip, who turned out to be something of a character. Charlie Budd showed up that first morning looking like he'd been beaten with the ugly-stick. Someone had kicked him in the face the night before. Apparently, prohibition didn't work any better in Sturgeons in 1968 than it had in Chicago in 1928. The locals just made their own hooch, which was a concoction that our guide described as "wicked." Anyone with eyes could see that Charlie Budd was a man suffering deeply from both a beating and a hangover.

First thing in the morning, after Quint and I got a good, solid sleep, this Charlie guy shows up looking like a carcass. Quint and I just rolled with it—what else could we do?

"Mornin', I'm Charlie," he said.

"I'm Quint, this is Gary." We all shook hands.

We soon learned that Charlie was a man of very few words. "Ken told me you need a guide to get a moose."

"Yes, are you our guide?" I asked.

"Yeah. Let's go." And that was that.

Charlie managed to get us into the woods and set up on a couple mounds of sawdust, and then he took off, not to be seen until high noon. I suspected he might have been trying to sleep off some of last night's hooch. We didn't see any game on the trail that morning at all. When Charlie staggered back to us around lunchtime, all he brought for our lunch was a can of Spam, dry bread, and black tea. Apparently this was a no-frills kind of place.

The key to hunting big game like elk, deer, and moose, is to hunt during the rut, when the animals are sexually active. The females go into estrus, which in turn gets the males pretty rutty. In Minnesota, where I've hunted my whole life, the rut is usually around November first. The peak of the first rut lasts about a week. Conservationists are well-tuned to rutting times of various species. They want to tightly control animal populations by adjusting the hunting seasons according to the rutting seasons.

During the rut, the males make scrapes with their feet and rub with their antlers against trees and such to let other males know they've been in the area, but it's not because they're territorial. It's more like a teenager tagging a train; they just want to put their mark on things. Most males of most species will go on the prowl, looking for a cute girl they can call their own, but they're generally looking for a good time, not a long time.

There are several ways to attract bulls of any species. For bull elk, I've found that the most effective call is to imitate a cow elk; sometimes referred to as a chirp call. I don't generally use a bull elk bugle because it can scare off any satellite bull elk you may want to shoot.

For bull moose, I have found that the most effective draw is to use a voice cow-call through a funnel-shaped megaphone that's about one or two feet long. Bull moose have extremely sensitive hearing because their antlers act as sound amplifiers. Once when I was in Alaska, my guide used a cow call, and it took a full 20 minutes for a bull moose with a 56-inch rack to find us—he was that far away.

Another effective draw for big game is to pour water out of a bucket from a height of about four feet, which simulates a cow peeing. Also, you can beat a canoe paddle against branches to simulate a moose moving through bush. If you're after moose, it helps to know that they don't have the best eyesight, so you can wave a couple of pail lids in the air to simulate horn movement.

Now, no one has ever accused me of being overly intuitive, but both Quint and I sensed that Charlie just wasn't that into the hunting. It might have been that he spent more time looking at his shoes than the trees, or it could have been that for much of that day he was probably sleeping it off. A lack of enthusiasm about hunting is generally not a quality one looks for in a hunting guide.

Quint, deciding that Charlie just needed a little motivation, said to him, "Charlie, I'll tell you what . . ." Charlie's chin came off his chest and he squinted at Quint with his one good eye. "If anyone—I mean me, Gary, or even you—bags a moose today, I'm gonna give you a twenty-five-dollar bonus."

Twenty-five bucks in 1968 was a lot of money. Charlie's one good eye bulged, and he treated us to a smile that exposed an incomplete set of very yellow teeth. "Sounds good!" he said, and immediately dove into his pack and came out with another can of Spam.

Quint cocked his head to the side, as in, *What now?*

Charlie snapped the key off the can and started bending it into a shell-ejecting device. Evidently, he'd broken the ejection pin on his gun and this was Charlie's fix. It worked well enough but meant that he only had a single-shot rifle. Not so good for moose hunting. He abruptly stood up, which must have hurt, judging by the pain on his swollen face, grabbed his rifle and pack, and took off like a man possessed. That was the last we saw of Charlie until supper.

After our Spam-and-bread lunch, I was having a lot of thoughts about a nice, hot supper. I conjured up all kinds of pictures in my mind about roasted, dripping meats; colorful, steaming vegetables; and freshly baked bread. Yum! By the time we got back to the village, my stomach was growling like a wolf at a bear. Quint and I sat down in the cookhouse, and as we were waiting for our dinner, I looked out the window and noticed a worker carrying a big ring of bologna across the yard. A small pack of mongrel dogs stalked him, all yipping, licking, and nipping at the sausage he was trailing. I thought to myself, *Hmm . . .* And sure enough, a half-hour later, that very same dog-licked bologna turned up on my plate.

The cuisine went downhill from there. The next morning, I found a runny egg on a piece of white bread. I grew up on a farm and learned to despise runny eggs from a young age. I hate 'em more than a head cold. Runny yolks and snotty whites. My inner culinary-critic gave it four black holes.

Charlie Budd joined us for what passed as breakfast that morning. I noticed that his appetite, unlike mine, was just fine. Ken the Caucasian joined us as well, and he had a piece of information that proved valuable.

"The mail plane was in this morning," he said. "I got talking with the pilot and told him that we had a couple of moose hunters staying with us."

"Oh yeah?" I said, wondering where he was going with this.

"Yeah, he told me that he spotted some moose on his flight in this morning," he said.

"No kidding! Where?" I asked, excited.

"He says they're on the other side of the lake," he replied.

Charlie looked up from his plate with one-and-a-half eyes,

his scraggly beard catching some of the yolk dripping off his fork, "Where?" he repeated, wanting more detail.

"On the southwest end of the southwest peninsula, close to the narrows," said Ken.

Charlie frowned and slowly shook his head. I asked, "That sounds great, so why the long face, Charlie?"

"Can't get there by land from here. Don't think the ice is thick enough to cross," he said.

"How far away is it?" I asked.

"'Bout 10 miles as the crow flies," he said.

"And if we hiked around?" I asked.

"'Bout 20-25 miles. But it's mostly heavy bush and snow. We couldn't do it in a day, that's for sure," he said. "It's better if we keep trying around here."

I deferred to his expertise and conceded the point. We finished up our small meal and headed out for day two of hunting around Namew Lake, but like the day before, we saw no moose and precious little sign. The weekend was closing, and we wanted our moose! That night both Quint and I spoke to Charlie about crossing the lake to where they'd been sighted. We wore him down until he reluctantly agreed. We'd leave before dawn to have a look at the ice.

The next morning, dark and early, Charlie picked us up with a snowmobile and an attached sled, and we all headed for Namew Lake. Temperatures had been below freezing for quite a while, so the lake was covered in ice and snow. Charlie drove the snowmobile out about 300 feet, stopped and dismounted. Wordlessly, he rummaged in his pack and came up with a hatchet, which he used to make a hole in the ice. It turned out to be six inches thick: plenty strong enough for a snowmobile and a sled. Charlie grunted approval, so we all piled back onto the snowmobile with the sled in tow.

On a lake that's so big you can't see the other side, snow doesn't usually fall and settle like a blanket. Rather, it blows across the ice and forms large drifts. It piles up in some areas and leaves bald ice in others. Exposed, clear ice looks a lot like open water. Furthermore, there are things called pressure ridges. There are two kinds of pressure ridges: overlapped and folded. The overlapped pressure ridges are relatively easy to spot because when one large sheet of ice pushes against another, one will overlap the other, leaving a pile of broken ice lined up down the length of the overlap. Folded ridges are harder to see. They form when the two masses of ice buckle instead of overlap. They're harder to spot because there is no pile of ice, only a bit of a hump or a dip, and the ice around them is thin, making them quite deadly. They can look a lot like a snow drift or an innocent bald spot when you're boogying along on a snowmobile in the dark, early dawn. Driving over one of those, or finding a thin spot on the lake, would make for a seriously bad day at best, and at worst, well . . .

"There!" I would shout and point to a shiny spot ahead of us. Charlie would slow the vehicle down, and we'd cautiously approach the spot. Is it a ridge? Is it a soft spot? Or, is it just bare ice six inches thick?

"Bald spot," Charlie would declare, and we'd move on until the next one.

"There!" shouted Quint, pointing to a jagged line on the horizon, caught in our headlights. Again, Charlie slowed down and carefully approached.

"Pressure ridge," he said, and turned us parallel to it at a distance he judged safe. That sucker was between six and 10 feet wide! We had to follow it for half a mile before we could safely get across. I was glad we spotted it before it ate us whole.

At daybreak, we finally reached the peninsula. Surely the moose would still be there. Surely. We started with the assumption that there were moose on the narrow peninsula, which was about two-miles long and only 300-600 yards wide. The game plan was to drive the moose toward the end of the peninsula. Quint would position himself about half-way down. Charlie and I would start at the base and move toward the point, hopefully causing the moose to also move toward the point. Then, Quint could either block or shoot the moose.

After hunting for the better part of the day, I finally spotted just the leg of a moose through the thick timber but had no clear shot at the vitals. A few minutes later I heard a shot from Charlie's gun. Less than a minute after that, or just long enough for the Spam key to work, I heard a second shot. I headed over to where I heard the sound to see what we had. Sure enough, there was Charlie standing at the head of the huge beast, grinning wide, giving us a great view of those dentals!

"Good one!" I shouted.

"Yup. He's a big one," said Charlie, pride clear on his face. "Recon he's gotta be 'bout 900 pounds."

Not long later, Quint appeared and we all congratulated ourselves on filling a tag and getting our prize. Then we got down to the business of gutting and preparing the carcass for travel.

"We'll come back for it in the morning," said Charlie.

"What are you talking about?" asked Quint. "We have to get it back to the village tonight."

Charlie looked at the sky, "No, it's going to be dark soon. We can't drag the sled through the bush to load the whole carcass, so we got to bring it out in pieces. There's not enough time to make all those trips to the sled."

Quint insisted. "I don't want to leave it out overnight for the wolves and scavengers. Besides, we need to leave tomorrow. In the morning, we won't have time to come back over the lake, load it up, get back across the lake again, and then drive all the way back to Rochester in time for work. No. We have to do this now."

"Be midnight before we get it all loaded. Then we still got to get over the lake," said Charlie.

"We don't have to butcher it all here. We'll just finish the gutting and use the snowmobile to drag the whole carcass back to the sled," said Quint.

Charlie's good eye rounded and even the still-swollen one looked sceptical, "You think the snowmobile can haul the whole thing through the bush?"

"Sure," said Quint, "if the three of us help it along and we get a move-on. What do you think, Gary?"

I looked at the huge animal lying on the ground and had my doubts, but Quint was right. We were on a deadline. "Well, we can sure try," I said.

"Okay," said Charlie, dubiously shaking his head. He went back to the work of cleaning the moose's innards. To my surprise, he laid his rain coat down on the snow beside the moose and then scooped most of the guts into it. He collected absolutely everything except for the large stomach: the "bum gut."

I found some coagulated blood on the frozen ground and helpfully kicked it in his direction, "You want that too?" I asked.

He grunted, "Nope." I grinned. He rolled up his goodie bag and said, "Let's go."

"Okay. Quint, you want to stay here with the moose while we get the snowmobile?" I asked.

"Will do," he said.

Charley and I hiked back to the lake where we'd left the snowmobile. He unhooked the sled and we drove just the machine back to Quint and the moose.

Back in the '60s, they built snowmobiles quite simply.

This one had a short track with several bogie wheels (the small wheels the tracks roll on). It probably had a small, 15-horsepower Kohler. It was heavy, though. Carbon fiber wasn't the material of choice on those machines yet. Still, considering the rough terrain, it did a marvelous job.

When we got back to the moose, we secured it by the nose to the rear hitch with a short piece of rope and off we went. We dragged the carcass through troughs and over boulders, around trees and over stumps. Several times we got bogged down in the brush or had to navigate a fallen tree, we even lost a few of the bogie wheels, but we made it back to the lake just as night was falling. It took all three of us on the front end of the moose to grunt it up onto the edge of the sled, and then all three of us on the back end to slide it all the way in. I was gasping for air by the time we had it loaded. Each breath hit the cold air and turned thick white. Ice formed around my nostrils, and my lungs burned. With no time to waste, Charlie got on the snowmobile, while Quint and I climbed on top of the moose for a nice, warm seat home.

If the trip over was scary, the trip back was terrifying. There was no moon and the night was absolute, save the thin light from our headlight. We still had to contend with the snow drifts. Bald ice spots still fooled us. We still knew there was a man-eating overlap pressure ridge out there somewhere—at least one that we knew of for certain. Only now, we were hauling the extra weight of a 900-pound moose.

My imagination can be a beautiful or terrible thing. That night, it was terrible. I could just see us going down with the rig. I could hear my good friend Quint crying out in the night, the whine of the tracks underwater as they lost traction. Then, the loss of sound and light as we all sank to the bottom of the black lake. The water would freeze above us, and our bodies would be entombed, never to be found. Truly, I died a thousand times out there on the lake, in the dark. When we finally spotted the glittering light of the village about three miles away, I felt the first twitch of hope. Three excruciating miles later, we pulled into the village, riding high atop our kill.

I did not realize that getting a moose in that village was going to be such a big deal. Charlie was like the football captain after an end-of-season win. We must have resembled Santa Claus. People descended on us like children after presents.

"Can I take the liver?"

"Can I have the heart?"

"Can we have the ribs?"

"I will make a good stew with that kidney."

We were lucky to get away with as much meat as we did. Still, we had a full load on top of the car carrier, and more in the trunk.

That night, we had one last meal of dog-licked bologna with Charlie. Quint said, "Well Charlie, I had my doubts about you when you showed up with that shiner and a hangover, but you came through for us."

"Yup. Got the job done," said Charlie, grinning that crook-ed-tooth grin.

"I know I told you I'd give you a bonus if you helped us bag a moose a couple days ago, but I guess today is close enough," he said, pulling out his wallet and extracting the bills.

One last time, Charlie treated us to his appalling dental hygiene as he took the money. I shook his hand and thanked him. Then, after the meal, Quint and I walked over to see Ken the Caucasian and settle our bill. In conversation, we mentioned that we tipped Charlie 25 bucks.

"That's good," said Ken. I thought he was glad for Charlie's sake, but then he added, "It'll end up in my cash register before the end of the day." He smiled large.

Sure enough, not 10 minutes later, one of Charlie's kids came into the store and bought a Coleman lantern. I was just glad it didn't go to any more of that wicked hooch.

The road out was just as pitted and grooved as it was on the way in, only now we had the added weight of the moose and the clearance was nearly nil. We had a careful, bumpy ride back to the world of pavement and double lines, but it was filled with a lot of newly minted, fond memories. It was interesting to see such a vastly different culture, and how white men had changed it: for better and for worse. Still, the remoteness of the area and its associated challenges made us decide to stay a little closer to home next time.

● ● ● ●

3 • BOUNDARY WATERS CANOE AREA

THE BOUNDARY WATERS CANOE AREA is an area of wilderness tucked into the northeast corner of Minnesota. It spans some of the northwest shore of Lake Superior and shares a border with Ontario, Canada. Minnesota preserved the first 500,000 acres back in 1902, and today, there are 1,090,000 acres of protected forest, lakes, and waterways.

My wife, Ginny, and I drove up to enjoy some camping and fishing. Despite dodging a grader and visiting a ditch, it had been a good day. I was out and breathing the clean air of the wilderness. There's something about wilderness air that makes me feel fully alive. It was around dusk when everything around me seemed to slow right down. Sensing the change, I stopped to see; to listen. The water on the lake stilled and became a clear mirror for the sky. The sun settled in behind the trees, and the trees lost all color, preferring to be silhouettes for a time. The final wisps of daylight reflected in the lake between dark patches of cloud and deep, universe blue. As the blue turned to black, and even the lowest light dimmed to darkness, the whole world seemed to hold its breath.

And then—the haunting cry of a single loon broke the silence. Low and mournful, she called to her mate, "I'm here!" Then, in perfect two-part harmony, he joined her call with his own, "I'm here!" The two-part harmony became three with another loon calling her soulmate, and then four-part with his

17

reply. Soon a dozen loons were all singing the same love song. I listened long into the night. Lying there with my beautiful wife, in our tiny little tent; I was one with creation and utterly filled with joy.

● ● ● ●

4 • GOOD SHOOTIN' DEAR

NOW, I'M CERTAIN THAT EVERY good newlywed man would agree that it's a great idea to take his new bride hunting. (Right?) I did a good job of selling her on its joys and challenges, and Ginny, being Ginny, was game to give it a try.

Ginny stands 5' 4" and weighs 110 pounds soaking wet, but she's a powerhouse physically, mentally, emotionally, and spiritually.

I set her up with all the proper gear including the required red clothing. No one had thought of blaze-orange back then.

"You look great in red," I said admiringly.

She smiled coyly and said, "Well, thank you."

Man, I was so in love.

I remember the black-and-white striped sweater she wore the first day I met her. I was supposed to go on a blind date with her roommate, but the roommate got sick and I got Ginny. When I was 19, and she was 21, I simply had to marry her. We've been together for 56 years, so I think it might stick. Looks permanent!

However, I digress.

We were hunting deer, so I gave her a 12-gage pump slug gun. She handled it alright during shooting practice, but I secretly hoped that the recoil wouldn't kick her right out of the tree stand. We woke up well before dawn on a fine, crisp November morning and hiked deep into a 60-acre stand of woods.

When we found a really good spot, we set up a tree stand and she climbed onto it. I still had plenty of time to find my own tree and set up a stand before the sun came up.

"Stay here until I come to get you," I said.

"I'm not going anywhere," she said.

I followed the well-traveled game trail for about a quarter mile until I came across the perfect oak tree. I was close enough to Ginny that I could keep an eye on things, and I still had a great view of the trail. I climbed up about 10 feet and settled onto my own stand. It was a perfect morning—the kind where you can feel the cool, clean air nourishing your cells. I watched the dark sky slowly turn from midnight black to outer-space blue, and then a thin line of light-orange appeared on the horizon. I was deeply into the morning meditation when the crack of a gunshot snapped me back to attention. It had come from Ginny's direction. I didn't hear a second shot, so I figured she probably missed. I was in a perfect position and had spotted fresh sign on the hike in, so I decided to stay put for a while longer rather than go back to her.

Another hour on guard did not bring forth the deer I saw earlier, nor any other game, so I decided to go and check on Ginny. I took a different route back to her, which brought me onto a road. There, I saw a guy hunched over a beautiful 10-point buck that he had gutted and was trying to drag to his truck. This kill must have been the shot I'd heard earlier.

"Hey buddy," he said when he saw me.

"How're you doing?" I said. "That's a beauty! What's that, 10 points?" It was a great buck, bigger than anything I'd ever shot.

"Sure is," he replied. He stopped tugging on the deer for a moment and took a hard look at me. I guess I must have looked harmless enough because he said, "You mind giving me a hand getting this in?" He nodded at his truck.

"Yeah, no problem," and together we grunted the big animal into the back of his pickup. We chatted for a while, shook hands and he drove away.

When I finally got back to Ginny's tree, I found her still sitting eight feet up on the stand, but she was nearly vibrating with excitement.

"Gary! Where have you been? I got one! I shot a buck! It was huge!" she said.

"You got one? No kidding? Where is it?" I looked around.

"Get me down from here, I'll show you. It went that-a-way."

"That's great Ginny! Where exactly did you shoot it?" I asked as I helped her out of the tree.

"Right here," she pointed to a location about 75 feet from us.

"No," I said, walking to the spot she pointed to, "I mean, where did the bullet enter the deer?"

"Oh, about here," she indicated that she got it just behind the shoulder blade, center mass, into the lungs. A perfect shot.

"Well, with that kind of a shot, he shouldn't be too far away. They don't always pile up in a heap. Sometimes they'll run for a while," I said. "We'll have to go find him—fast."

"A man came by though," she said with a furrowed brow.

"A man? When?"

"Not long ago, maybe 40 minutes."

"What did he want?" I asked.

"He asked me if I'd seen any game. I told him I had a good shot at a buck not long ago. I showed him the blood trail and he went to follow it, so I got out of the stand and followed him," she said.

"What happened?" I asked.

"Well," Ginny looked confused and said, "he found the buck right away, but he said he was the one who shot it. I told him that I was the one who shot it. But . . ." she trailed off.

"But what?"

"But he said that the bullet hole is always bigger on the exit side than the entry side, so it couldn't have been me who shot it because of the way the bullet holes were, so I just came back to the tree stand to wait for you."

"He told you WHAT?" I cried, shocked.

"It is malarkey . . . right?" she asked, not sure.

"Yes. It's a total load of malarkey. You shot the deer. The blood trail starts from where you shot it and led to where it lay. YOU shot that deer!" I told her. "Come on," I said and started along the path that had been trampled now by a bleeding deer, a man, and my wife—twice.

We crashed through the bush, following the trail as quickly as we could until we came to a gut pile. It took me about a nanosecond to know what I'd already guessed: I had just helped some guy steal the buck that Ginny shot. I was steaming.

"That rotten, low-down . . ." I turned heel and started walking. "I can't believe he did that! I can't believe I did that!"

"What do you mean?" she asked, "What did you do?"

"I helped the thief steal your buck, that's what I did!" I just couldn't believe it.

As we walked back to her tree stand, I told my part of the story. We gathered our gear, got back to the car, and drove into Carlos. Based on what the guy had said to me back in the woods as I helped him load his booty, I was able to find his house. Sure enough, there was his pickup truck in the driveway. I climbed the front steps, with Ginny in hot pursuit, and banged on the door. What followed was a serious butt chewin'.

"What do you think you're doing? You didn't shoot that deer!" I nearly yelled the moment he opened the door.

"I don't know what you're talkin' about," he said, backing up, "I shot it myself!"

"You know darn well you didn't shoot that buck. My wife

22

shot it. You followed the blood trail from *where she* shot it and then lied to her about how *you* shot it. Did she tell you it was her fist time hunting?" I challenged.

He shifted his weight from one foot to the other as his gaze flickered from my nearly purple face to Ginny standing behind me. "Well what of it?" he asked.

"What of it? What of it? Is that why you handed her all that malarky about entry and exit wounds? You figured she didn't know any better and you could get away with the lie! You're a liar and a thief, and you took advantage of my wife's lack of knowledge, and then you lied to me, too. You had the nerve to get me to help you load it, knowing full well it wasn't yours to take!"

"Get off my property!" he cried. "Get off my property before I call the cops!"

"Go ahead! Call them! We'll see who the criminal is here!" I was beyond angry and was ready take on an army singlehanded, but then I felt Ginny touch my elbow and heard her speak to the little rodent in her strongest voice.

When Ginny uses that voice, people listen. Period.

"You Sir, know what you did and you're going to have to live with that. We're going to leave now, but I hope you think long and hard about the way you treat others and the way you're living your life. I will pray for you."

She was right, I knew there wasn't much point in arguing with the man. He stole and lied, and he'd have to live with the guilt of that. I turned on the stoop, but before stepping down I couldn't help myself and added, "I hope you get indigestion with every bite of that deer you take." And that was that.

It was the first and last time Ginny ever hunted. The next year we were into babies. I could understand her decision. Still, she would have made a terrific hunter considering that she made a perfect shot into a buck bigger than anything I'd ever shot. It was a shame to lose a potentially great hunting partner, but at least I still had her as a great life partner.

● ● ● ●

5 • FARM LESSONS

I WAS BORN IN 1942 and grew up on a farm in Minnesota. I had a prayer warrior for a mother and a kind-hearted hard worker for a father. My sister, Marlys, is 10 years older than I am. My brother, Don, is seven years my senior. Even though I feel close to them, I never had a sibling close to me in age, so I spent a fair amount of time on my own when I was a kid. But that was okay by me. My favorite book in grade school was *The Lone Cowboy*. I would imagine sleeping out under the stars in the Wild West with a bed roll for lying on and a saddle for a pillow. I've always enjoyed being by myself.

With cows, horses, and chickens to take care of on the farm, I rarely had to look for something to do. The hard work of tending to livestock taught me to do the hard work of living a good life. Going to church and respecting the Word taught me to be thankful for all that I'm so blessed with.

One of my jobs was to gather the fresh eggs daily. Every now and then I would forget, and when I did, whoa! Did I ever regret it! I would go into the chicken coop the next day and find that the hens had managed to crush their own eggs and make a disgusting gooey mess of the straw nests, which I then had to clean out. I also had to clean the cement-like goop off the eggs that managed to stay in one piece.

Note to self: remember to gather the eggs every day.

Lesson learned: be accountable.

Forgetting or shirking on a farm just wasn't an option. You forget to milk a cow and she got milk fever: real suffering. You accidentally let a cow get loose and eat all the fresh fodder she wants, and she'll bloat: more suffering. Back in 1949, my dad needed surgery on his back, so he turned the farm over to my uncle, Elmer, for one year. While Dad was in the hospital, a cow got loose and bloated on too much alfalfa. Ma warned me not to tell my dad when he came home because she didn't want him to get too stressed out. Of course, the day he came home, he no more than got out of the car when I shouted, "Hey dad, there's a dead cow out there in the field!" Fortunately, he took it well. The cow paid a far greater price for that mistake than my dad did. Still I learned the lesson: when you don't pay attention, or when you don't do the chores, you get instant negative results.

Note to self: pay attention to others.

Lesson learned: shirking leads to suffering.

The chickens were my enemies. I just really, really hated the chickens. If I wasn't cleaning up broken eggs, I was taking abuse from a rooster. One day, on the way to pick eggs, a rooster figured I had invaded his territory. Bravely, but not wisely, he decided to rush me and peck my leg. It hurt!

"Get off!" I shouted at the angry little bird. I kicked out, but it just kept coming at me. The injury added to the insult was just too much to take. The next day, I brought my softball. Again the rooster rushed my leg, but this time I pitched that ball like a pro and knocked the rooster right off his feet.

"Hah!" I shouted. "You don't want to play hardball with me!" Unfortunately, I ended up killing the bird. Upon discovering this, I ran as quickly as my little legs could carry me to the tool shed, grabbed a shovel, and before a hanging-judge can shout "Guilty!" I had that rooster buried behind the chicken coop, never to be heard from again. My parents were kind and probably would have just made a chicken dinner out of it, but I had no intention of telling anyone about that bird. No way was I going down for being chicken of a rooster.

Note to self: bury the bodies well.

Lesson learned: it's okay to defend yourself, but try not to kill anything over it.

It's probably fair to say that I also discovered, at a very young age, that I did not want to become a farmer, at least not a dairy farmer. I had been suspecting it for some time, but the clincher came one hot August day when my dad left me alone to milk the cows. The cows were in stanchions, so they couldn't move while I milked them, and they stood on a low platform, so that anything emitted from their hind ends would land in a deep gutter for easy shovelling later. I had just unhooked a surge milking machine from a cow and had to walk around the back of her to get to the next cow. I carefully avoided the gutter and was minding my feet when—SLAP! The stinkin' cow hit me right across the face with her tail that was dripping with urine.

"Aaaaahhhh!" I yelled, causing all the cows to jump a little. I ran to the faucet we had in the barn, turned it on full-blast, and stuck my whole head under the water. I scrubbed my face, my hair, my neck, my ears—everything—and then I scrubbed it all three more times. I was under the water for what seemed like a half-hour. As I shook the water out of my hair, I thought, *Ya know, there's got to be a better way to make a buck.*

Note to self: if you only look at your feet, you won't see the wet tail coming.

Lesson learned: be careful about going behind someone's back.

It wasn't all hard, though. One of the best lessons I ever learned on the farm was to appreciate the great outdoors and enjoy all of creation. After a hard day of summer work, grimy with dust and sweat, we'd sometimes pile into the car and head for Lake Irene. Jumping into that cool water and scrubbing off the day's labor was so refreshing that I remember it vividly these many years later. I remember diving under the water and scrubbing my scalp until it tingled. I remember swiping a hand down my leg and leaving a clean streak. I was smooth and pale, except where the scratches and bruises of a good, lived life left their marks. Even back then, in the moment, I felt grateful. Now, as I look back on many years of life, I am more grateful than ever. I'm blessed with an appreciation for farming, for lakes and forests; for fish and game; for a good career; for my two great kids, Dawn and Troy; and for my awesome wife, Ginny. She's been my partner and love who has supported me in all my ventures: business and recreational.

● ● ● ●

Shocking oats with my dad, brother, and sister.
That's me in front, being shocking.

28

6 • THE PIG

OUR FIRST CHILD, DAWN, WAS born in 1966. She was like a little miracle that drove me to study even harder. I spent a year at vocational school before going on to work for the lawn mower company, Toro. I wasn't there long before I decided to go to work for IBM in Rochester, Minnesota.

Once, not far from home, on a warm and clear November day in the early '60s, I was enjoying a pheasant hunt with my boss at IBM, Mike. He was half Polish and half Russian. He was quite a guy: fought in WWII for the Polish army, went to England, then to Sweden, and eventually found his way to the States and the University of Minnesota. Mike rarely met a topic he didn't have an opinion about, and he wasn't shy about telling you what it was.

Anyway, on this beautiful day in Minnesota corn country, we were hunting for pheasant and we came across a pig farm, which is inevitable when you're in Minnesota corn country. Back then, the barns were smaller than they are now, and they were a part of the more traditional farms. It was quite idyllic. Farmers had planted the gently rolling hills with deep-green fields of corn. White farm houses and red outbuildings nestled into groves of leafy trees throughout the countryside. Cows grazed, chickens roamed freely, and pigs perfumed the air. Well, maybe not *perfumed*, exactly.

Seeing the pigs in their pens apparently put Mike in mind

of a pig roast. He had visions of turning a hog on a spit and then serving it with a nice, red apple in its mouth. His visions were so compelling that when we came across a young farm boy, he asked about the pigs.

"How much do you want for one of those little piglets?" asked Mike.

The boy, maybe 14 or 15 years old, gave him a price, and then boldly stood his ground.

"What?" cried Mike, eyes sparking. "Are you farming or robbing? That price is so steep I'll need climbing gear to pay it!" The haggling was on! "You feeding those pigs lobster and champagne? Do they have royal pedigrees or something?"

"Mister, you never tasted pork like you're going to taste with these honeys! When you taste these pigs, you'll wish you paid me double!" And so it went.

Finally the two businessmen came to an agreement. Mike paid the boy and they agreed that he could return to the farm to pick out a piglet at some future date. We carried on with our pheasant hunt and soon forgot all about the piglets.

Several weeks later, Mike decided that it was a good time to go and retrieve his piglet. He asked me to butcher it. He said, "Connie's out of town for a few days. We'll go and pick the best of the litter, bring it home and butcher it up at the house."

"That sounds like a good plan," I said. "No problem," I said. "Sure thing," I said.

I had watched my dad and his brother, Elmer, butcher pigs before. It didn't look too hard, so I figured I could manage it without much trouble. I was a farm boy after all. How difficult could it be?

How naïve could I be?

We drove out to the farm and knocked on the door of the white, two-story house. A nice looking, middle aged woman wearing an apron and sensible shoes opened the door. We introduced ourselves and explained that we were there to collect a piglet.

"Why yes, I remember Aaron telling me about you," she said with a little smile that made me wonder just what Aaron had told her. It had been quite the haggle, but I had a notion that the boy came away the winner. "He's out slopping the pigs right now as a matter of fact. You'll find him in the hog barn. You'll need to drive about a quarter mile down that road there. Go on around, you'll find him."

We thanked her and climbed back into Mike's brand-new Ford Falcon. We drove past the main barn, standing high and painted proud red. Then we got to the hog barn. They'd painted it the same proud red, but the reek of pig manure gave its function away. Sure enough, when we walked up to the pens, we spotted the boy we'd met earlier.

"Aaron!" Mike called, leaning against the pen.

"Well hey Mike! How are you doing?" Aaron said, strolling over casually, and shaking both of our hands. Mike surreptitiously wiped his hand off behind his trousers.

"Guess you've come for your pig?" Aaron said.

"Yup. Have you got a good one for me?" asked Mike.

"Sure do! Come and take your pick. As you can see, they've grown some since you were here last."

That was an understatement. The cute little pigs that had crowded around a heavy sow, each pushing for a turn at the teat, had grown halfway into real hogs. Maybe they actually were feeding them lobster and champagne.

Mike, always wanting to get his money's worth, wanted to feed as many guests as he could, so he looked over the herd of swine and pointed at the biggest one.

"Yeah, figgers," Aaron said. Then he looked to me and said, "You wanna go get that gunny sack hanging on the wall just inside the barn door for me?"

I walked over to the hog barn and took down the burlap sack hanging where he'd pointed. A hog barn sure does stink. I brought it back to the pen just in time to watch the entertainment.

Aaron had taken up a feed bucket and was trying to coax the pig over. The pig wasn't having any of it. It was like it knew. The boy might have had 40 or 45 pounds on the young pig, but the pig was wily. I gave them even odds.

"Heeeer pig pig pig pigpigpig! Heeeer pig pig pig pigpigpig!" Aaron gently called.

"Not a chance," said the pig.

For each step Aaron took forward, the pig took one back. I knew pigs were smart. Teenaged boys, maybe not so much. Aaron lunged at the pig, which neatly dodged left, leaving Aaron on his hands and knees in the slop. Mike snorted. I covered my mouth.

Aaron got one hand on a knee to push himself up but the foot taking the weight slipped out from under him and he plopped back down, nearly doing the splits. Mike whooped. I started shaking.

The pig had taken refuge behind his siblings now, so Aaron had to wade into the crowd. He started toward a smaller pig when Mike called out, "No, not that one. The big one!" Aaron flicked an annoyed glance our way but redirected his attention to the big one again. He still had hold of the slop pail which nearly every pig in the pen showed an interest in, except for the big one. Aaron gave up and let the others have it, so he could concentrate on the prize.

"Heeeer pig pig pig pigpigpig," Aaron coaxed.

"Go away," came the snorted reply.

Again, Aaron lunged and again the pig dodged left, leaving Aaron lying flat out in mud and excrement. He uttered a few words that I imagine his mother might not have approved of.

Mike and I had tears running down our cheeks by that time. I doubled over, and Mike's face was turning an alarming shade of purple as he wheezed with laughter. When Aaron managed to find his feet, he turned and glared at us—then I completely lost it.

Finally, the boy cornered the pig. This time, Aaron wised up, when he lunged at it he veered to his right at the last second. The pig dodged left again but this time Aaron grabbed its hind leg. Squealing bloody murder, the pig went down. It tried to kick off its captor, but Aaron was embarrassed and determined.

"Grab the gunny sack!" he shouted.

Mike grabbed the bag and we rushed around the pen to help. I reached through the fence and took hold of the pig's front legs. Mike managed to get the sack over its head. Together we got the beast into the gunny sack and tied it shut. Then Mike carried it over to the Falcon and threw it in the trunk.

"Good work," said Mike.

"Yeah. That was a job alright," I agreed, walking around to the passenger side. Aaron followed me and reached for the shiny, chrome door-handle of Mike's pride and joy.

"Stop right there," said Mike to Aaron.

"But . . ." Aaron looked dismayed. Then he looked down at himself, all covered in pig pen, looked at Mike's nice car, and nodded resignation.

Mike came around and stuck his hand out, "It was a pleasure doing business with you," he said. Then his eyes crinkled at the corners and his mouth tightened and he said, "Truly."

"Aww . . ." Aaron broke out in a wide grin and shook our hands. "Okay. Yeah. You take care."

I guess he walked the quarter of a mile home. We drove back to Mike's house.

Mike lived on the top of a hill in a very "Tony" part of Rochester.

It was the kind of place where people kept their lawns mowed and houses freshly painted. You could look down and see rows and rows of houses and the whole city lit up at night. It wasn't the kind of neighborhood where you'd find a live pig. Which we had. In the trunk. This posed a problem.

For good reason, Mike didn't want to fire his .22 in the front yard, so we needed to come up with another way of killing the pig.

"I've heard that slaughterhouses have a kind of hammer device. We could do it that way. It would be quieter. Do you have something like that?" I asked. Mike rummaged around the garage and came up with a carpenter's claw hammer.

"Will this work?" he asked.

"Should do," I said.

"You're just going to bludgeon it?" Mike asked.

"Yeah. It should only take one good hit," I said.

"Well, you go right ahead," he said, and handed me the hammer.

Thanks buddy.

We hauled the pig out of the trunk and I got a hold of its head. Then, I swung the hammer right between its eyes. The pig gave the worst squeal I've ever heard. I can still feel that squeal! It was awful. Quickly I swung again but that only caused it to squeal again but even louder, wouldn't you know it?

At this point, Mike couldn't take it anymore and he shouted, "!#@%* Gary! Stop tapping and HIT him!"

I beat on that pig like a rented mule. After several blows, the pig finally stopped squealing. We put a rope on each hind leg and got him hoisted up on the garage rafters, its front legs were a couple feet off the floor.

Mike, not wanting to waste a thing, decided he wanted to keep the pig's blood to make Polish sausage. He had an old recipe handed down from his mother.

THE PIG

"I haven't tasted it since I was in Poland," he said, his accent thickening with the memory.

"Okay, I can do that," I said, and Mike brought me a pan for the blood.

So, I stuck the pig in what I thought would be an artery but missed. I had no choice but to stab it again, and again, hoping to hit an artery. Finally, the blood started to gush, and I caught it in the pan. There is a reason for that expression, "bleeding like a stuck pig." Then, suddenly, the pig came to! It started to swing in circles with its front legs trying to run, and its hind legs hanging far above. So, there I was, chasing it in circles: One hand trying to catch blood in the pan and the other beating on it with a claw hammer. It had a lump on its head the size of an egg. After what seemed to be an eternity, the pig settled down and finally succumbed. The garage looked like a slaughterhouse.

Sweating, I finished filling up the pan and handed it over to Mike. Wide-eyed, he said, "Thank you," and took it into the kitchen where he would mix the blood with barley and feed it into the sausage stuffer. I placed another pan under the pig and sat down to rest.

After some time, the pig filled another entire container of blood. I wearily rose and carried the second pan into the house for Mike. I stopped in my tracks when I saw the kitchen. It looked like the site of a chainsaw massacre. Blood spattered the floor, the countertop, and even parts of the walls. Mike had drenched his shirt and trousers, and his face was spotted. The sausage was coming out nicely, but he forgot about a sharp knife on the counter that cut open the casings. More blood!

Mike saw me there, standing in the doorway with my mouth open, and he said, "Thank God Connie's not home." Yeah. If Connie had been home, I had no doubt that Mike wouldn't be eating sausage—he'd BE the sausage.

I went back into the garage, leaving Mike to his massacre, and started taking the hair off the pig and removing its entrails. As I worked, a small headache started just behind my eyes. By the time I finished butchering, my head was throbbing. The November day had turned cold and I was feeling done. That was when Mike came out with a toothbrush.

"What's that for?" I asked.

"The pig," he said.

"The pig?" I repeated.

"Yeah. The pig," he said. "I want to put an apple in its mouth.

"And you want me to—*brush its teeth?*" I was amazed.

"Would you?" He held out the toothbrush to me and I reluctantly took it.

"What? No toothpaste?" I asked sardonically, but it went past him.

"No, I don't want it to taste minty."

After that, I had such a brutal headache that I missed another three days of work.

The winter passed and eventually spring returned.

I was driving through the countryside one fine day when the memory of the piglet came back to me. He hadn't invited me to any pig feast over the winter and I wondered what ever became of the bacon. Should I ask? I decided I would.

The next time I saw Mike I said, "So Mike, how was the pig?"

"Oh, I didn't care for it," he replied nonchalantly.

I was stunned. "Huh," was all I could manage to say.

After all that work, all that pain, all that trauma! All he said was, "I didn't care for it"! At least he could have lied and said it was terrific! He could have said, "Not bad," or even, "The apple was great!"

But no. He "didn't care for it."

As one can well imagine, that first pig butchering was also my last.

● ● ● ●

It wasn't long after this incident that I decided a high school diploma wasn't enough. It was time to go back to school. I had been working at IBM and saw how the guys got pigeon-holed in their jobs, retired, and died—on average, about 16 months after retirement. I thought about that and decided it was safer to go back to school. Three years later I was a mechanical engineer.

● ● ● ●

7 • THE BEST LURES

I LEARNED A COUPLE OF things in Spirit Lake, Iowa. First, I learned that the definition of eternity is sitting at a four-way stop in Spirit Lake, Iowa. Second, just like you have to get onto the sidetracks to find the best game, you also need to get onto the sidetracks to find the best fishing lures.

Stanley Mingus, of Spirit Lake, Iowa made the best bucktail jigs I've ever used. I saved the hair from the tails of bucks I'd shot and brought it to Stanley's home. He worked out of his basement, but to see him, you first had to get past his wife. She could give you a look that would stop a train. Still, Stanley's jigs were well worth it.

"Stanley! How are you?" I asked one day, shaking his hand. As usual, I found him working on some lures, sharpening a jig to a needle point.

"Gary, good to see you," he said. "Where have you been fishing these days? Caught much?" Right to the point. Fishing lures were basically his life. I think the only time Stanley ever emerged from making lures in his basement was when he went to Okoboji Lake to test his lures. He'd stand on the bridge and usually catch his limit. He could make a bucktail jig look exactly like a minnow. The man was an artist.

"As a matter of fact, I have. That's what I wanted to come by and tell you," I said.

"Have a seat, have a seat," he removed several papers from

a chair and pulled it over to his workbench for me. He had the workbench covered in all manner of things: animal hair, feathers, beads, small tire weights, dyes, pliers, cutters, and a big magnifying glass.

I sat. "You remember those bucktail jigs you made for me last month?"

"Of course," he said.

"Well, I just got back from a hunting trip and got some fishing in too," I said.

"Shoot anything?" he asked.

"Yeah, a nice moose. I brought you some hair," I pulled a bag of moose hair out of my pocket and handed it over.

"Good. Very nice," he said, rolling the strands between his finger and thumb.

"The hunting was good, but I really wanted to tell you about this one day I was using your jigs to fish walleyes," I said.

Stanley pulled his attention from the moose hair and turned back to me. "Yeah?"

"I cast 13 times and caught 13 walleyes!" I declared.

"Well!" he laughed, "Can't beat that!"

"No sir! You can't beat that!" I agreed.

I bought several more lures from him, at three for a buck. A steal at twice the price.

Note to self: when you get a lead on someone who can tie a fly that well, it's best to forget about bait shops and stick with the sidetrack.

Sometimes, there just isn't a guy like Stanley around to tie your flies and you have to resort to the path more traveled. I remember, when I was a kid, I used to pour over Herter's Catalogs. I loved them! Not just for all the amazing and wonderful things that a person could buy, but for the sheer entertainment value of the writing.

Ethics weren't an issue for Herter. He claimed that the North Star Guides Association endorsed many of his products, but the North Star Guides Association didn't exist. He often co-wrote with Jacques P. Herter II or George L. Herter II—who didn't exist. Sometimes he'd trash-talk the competitors, and he even made a game of stealing their product ideas, changing them slightly, and then selling them cheaper. He wasn't subtle about it either. He reinvented Mepps Spinners and sold them in the catalog as Pepps Spinners. The Johnson Silver Minnow became Herter's Olson Minnow. Why spend money marketing when you can just piggyback off the competition?

Personally, I was often disappointed by the quality of the goods that I ordered. Merchandise that might have been worth 600 pages of POW, WOW, BAM advertising to Herter, was to me, worth about as much paper as a postcard. Give me Stanley Mingus's hand-tied flies any day.

However, the appeal of the catalog wasn't just the price of the goods sold. The articles George Herter wrote were outlandish and made me laugh time and again. I could spend hours looking at fishing gear and guns and clothing. I read them cover to cover. I learned a lot from those catalogs. I discovered a whole world of fishing and hunting gear that I otherwise would have had no way of knowing about. I also learned about the value of buying original versus knock-offs.

Note to self: don't believe everything you read.

● ● ● ●

8 • BUGGIN' OUT

I LEFT IBM IN 1964 and went back to school. In three years I'd earned my engineering degree. In 1967, I went to work for Rochester Datronics. There, I designed a mark-sensing computer that interpreted multiple-choice tests marked with a #2 pencil. In 1968, Ginny and I had our second child, Troy. Those were busy years filled with babies, work, church, and of course—in my case—fishing and hunting.

Al was a friend from our church group in Rochester who heard me talk about how beautiful it is in the Boundary Waters Canoe Area Wilderness and decided he wanted to see it for himself. Happy to have him along, a group of us headed to Knife Lake for some fishing over the Memorial Day weekend.

The BWCA is the kind of place where you either love it the first time, or you hate it. I fell in love with it right away, but my buddy, Al—he had a different experience.

We got the canoes into the water, piled them full of gear, and headed down the river. At the first portage, I noticed that he rolled up his sleeves.

"Al," I said, "did you put bug lotion on?"

"Naw," he replied. "I didn't bother. The bugs aren't that bad. Guess I'm just not sweet enough or something."

Having been to the lake enough times, I knew better. You might not see the no-see-ums and blackflies, but they'll see you, sweet or not. I said, "I've got some right here in my pack. I keep it close."

"Thanks Gary, I'm okay," he said.

You can lead a horse to water . . . I thought. My uncle Sven always said it differently: "You can lead a horse to drink, but you can't make him water."

Sure enough, about an hour later I saw Al clawing at his arms, his neck, his face, his hands, and pretty much anywhere he had exposed skin. He approached me. "Hey Gary?" He looked sheepish. "You, uh, you still have that bug lotion you mentioned?"

"Yeah, sure," I said, digging into my pack, and tossing him the bottle. "Keep it. Looks like you're plenty sweet," I nodded at his scratched-up arms. I always, always bring extra bug lotion with me on a trip.

That day went well. I remember the guys showed me a technique for baiting a line that I've used ever since. For bottom-feeding fish, or "lakers," I use frozen smelt as bait. Smelt has a GI tract that runs in a straight line from mouth to anus. I fashion a threader out of thin stove-pipe wire, with a hook at the end. I pass the threader through the mouth and out the anus, attach a loop made in the end of eight-pound monofilament line, and pull the whole unit back out through the mouth. I then attached a double hook to the line, so there is a hook on each side of the smelt's mouth. A half-hitch loop around its tail makes it secure and completes the rig. I cast out and the smelt slowly sinks to the bottom where it sits until a laker sees it.

But that's not the end of the story! The laker doesn't swallow the bait right away. It usually just carries it about 50-60 feet and thinks, *Hah! I got away with it!* and only then swallows the bait. Patience here is the key. If you feel the line quiver a little, you must give the fish the line, wait for the quivering to stop, and when you feel it move again, that's when you take up the slack and give the line a little tug to set the hook. At that point, the battle is on! With the rig we made, even a small five-pound lake trout would be a real fight from shore. It's great fun to think like a fish, only smarter.

By the end of the day, I had a pile of fish and was feeling quite satisfied. My buddy, Al, however, was swatting and swiping and scratching and smacking himself like a junkie in detox. The bug lotion wasn't having much of an effect. The poor guy stood, blinking and red-eyed, directly in the smoke of the campfire to get a break from them. When that didn't work very well, he simply took refuge in his tent and sleeping bag before the sun was even down.

The next morning, I climbed out of my tent, stretched, and yawned. The sun was just cresting the line of trees, and the birds were in full chorus. I felt fresh and rested and ready for another fun-filled day of fishing and camping. Al, however, was *not* a happy camper. He rose before me and had a fire going already. He was sitting in the smoke looking bleary and miserable.

"Gary," he said, "can you take me to that rock island out there?" pointing to a bare rock with no vegetation about 500 feet out into the lake.

"Um—sure," I said. "Mind if I ask why?"

"These BUGS!" he explained. "They're gonna kill me! I hafta get away from them before they eat me alive! Look at this," he rolled up the sleeve of his left arm to reveal a raw mass of bumpy, swollen flesh. As I looked, a mosquito landed. Al and I just stood there as we both watched in fascinated horror while it sucked Al's blood in exchange for its itchy deposit. Then, the mosquito, fat and red, withdrew its proboscis and exploded under Al's right hand.

"Yeah, let's go," I said.

By about 10:00 that morning I landed my third lake trout. Every now and then, I looked over to the island that we were all referring to as "Al's Rock." His idea of "sidetracks" was more about avoiding something bad than finding something good. At first, he paced, then he just sat for the longest time, slapping himself every so often, and then he got up and started to swing at the air like a crazy man. It was something to see. A guy standing on a bald rock in the middle of a lake, swatting and yelling at the air. I don't believe I've ever seen anyone get more excited about breaking camp and going home. The BWCA never saw Al again.

The bugs sure do miss him.

● ● ● ●

9 • PEOPLE OF THE BWCA

SOMETIMES IT'S GOOD TO GET away from the craziness of work and city life. The '60s were a busy time for me, so I took every opportunity I could to recharge my energy in the great outdoors. I'd pack my gear and head out to the Boundary Waters Canoe Area just to get away from it all. Still, every so often I came across other humans out there in the wild who were enjoying it all too.

One such time came when I spotted a couple of Indians on Monument Portage between Saganaga and Cypress Lakes. They were cooking on the smallest campfire I'd ever seen. It was just a whisper of smoke with a small pot hanging from a branch. Later, I saw them again when I was fishing in the rapids off the riverbank. They were in a 13-foot canoe they had loaded down with groceries. They were coming up on the rapids fast. It alarmed me because they were in a canvas canoe, not an aluminum one, and the rapids would make quick kindling out of it if they were to go over. It was with no small amount of relief that I saw them slow and then stop before plunging to their deaths. With a shake of my head, I reeled in my line and cast again.

When I looked back to the canoe, the guy in front had gotten out and was talking with the guy still sitting in the stern. It looked like a heated discussion with a lot of pointing and arm waving. From my vantage point, it looked like the guy in back wanted to take the canoe through the rapids, but the other guy wasn't having any of it.

If the suicidal guy still sitting in the canoe got his way, here's what would have happened. He would approach the rapids alone, with only one paddle for steerage. The rapids had a six-foot drop over 120 feet. He would start to speed up faster and faster and get caught in the current, so when he realized what a stupid thing he'd done, he'd already be past the point of no return. He'd be tossed from side to side, frantically paddling just to stay in the main current, but to no avail. He would inevitably smash into a boulder. He would be thrown into the air and fall into the maelstrom. He'd struggle to keep his head above water while the pieces of his boat swirled around. He'd grab out for things but there would be nothing to keep him afloat, and the current would take him down, where he would hit his head on an underwater rock, fall unconscious and drown. His buddy and I would hoof it downstream to recover the body that washed up on shore, along with a half-dozen boxes of cereal. My friends and I would then have one extra person and one dead body in camp. We'd have to canoe and portage them through four more sets of rapids before getting them to the truck. We'd drive them back to their families, who would be grief stricken, and it would all be very sad. No, I did not want that guy to shoot the rapids.

That whole scene played out in my mind in just a flash. The two men were still arguing. I felt a strong need to weigh in on the debate, so I began to wave my hands in a "go back" gesture, and a "go around by land" gesture. I don't know if they saw me, or if they did whether it made any difference, but the guy got out of the canoe. A wise decision.

Another year, a few of us were driving up for a moose hunt and we stopped to gas up. My moose-hunting buddy Quint brought along Lloyd, his brother-in-law, who was a veterinarian from Wisconsin. He was the kind of guy who wanted to know things; he liked details and asked a lot of questions. As we were gassing up, he got out of the car to stretch his legs and noticed a pickup truck with a bull moose in the box. He moseyed over to the truck to talk to the guy in the cab.

"Hey buddy, looks like a good-sized moose you have there," he said.

"Oui monsieur, ee's a beeg one," replied a French Canadian.

The reek of booze radiating off the man nearly knocked Lloyd off his feet, but he pretended not to notice the stink. (This was back when people didn't think of drinking and driving in the same way we do now.) "Must be a 55- or 60-inch spread?"

"Sixty-two!" declared the Frenchman proudly.

Lloyd, of course, was wondering if this was the kind of beast he could look forward to bagging on our trip, so he asked, "Where'd you get him?"

The drunk man slurred, "Right een the neck!"

Lloyd blinked a few times and then just laughed.

Not all people we met in the BWCA wilderness were crazy or suicidal or drunk; some were just plain tough. Dorothy Molter was one such character. I believe that woman could use shoelaces for dental floss! As tough as she was, though, she was equally friendly. Her day-job had been nursing in Chicago, but she left that behind her long ago. Now, her life was in the BWCA backcountry. She owned three islands in Knife Lake upon which she had built a few small cabins and one main cabin. She used broken canoe paddles to make a picket fence (her nod to traditionalism?), sold homemade root-beer to canoeists, and made friends with just about everyone.

One year, my buddy Quinton and his dad, Randy, found

themselves caught in a canoe in a snowstorm on the lake. This wasn't a common occurrence for Quint or Randy. Quint was an avid outdoorsman who was generally prepared for anything. In fact, he was not only my good friend, he was my hunting mentor, and his dad had been his hunting mentor. Quint was about 12 years my senior, stood 5' 8" but was quite overweight. He loved to cook, and he especially loved to eat. It would be diabetes that would eventually get the better of him and cause him to have to give up hunting. He was born and raised in Laporte, Minnesota, and was the friendliest guy you'd ever meet. Quint would give you the shirt off his back, his last dollar, and all the time in the world. He loved to talk to people and tell stories. He was genuine. Sadly, he passed away recently, but I still have nearly a lifetime of memories.

Quint later told me that as the snow kept coming down faster and thicker, he was getting worried. He felt like he was stuck in a snow globe. The flakes were big and wet, the kind that could bury you without a trace. The water on the lake was thickening up. It was time to find shelter. Fortunately, they were near Dorothy Molter's three islands. They paddled over, putting their backs into the work. They pulled the canoe up to Dorothy's little dock and tied up. His dad stayed with the canoe while Quint left to find the Lady of the island.

It was with relief that he spotted smoke rising out of the chimney of the main cabin, and when he knocked on the door Dorothy opened it without hesitation.

"Afternoon Dorothy," Quint said, removing his hunting cap.

"Quint? What are you doing out in weather like this? Good heavens! Come in, come in," she said in her customarily hospitable way.

Quint knocked the snow off his boots before stepping inside. When he did, he saw an old man lying on a cot just inside the door. Something about him looked off to Quint; like he was sick or something. There was a strange smell too, like something he'd smelled in a hospital before. Not all was right inside Dorothy Molter's world.

Looking away from the man, Quint said to Dorothy, "The storm caught us by surprise, I'm afraid. Dad's on the dock with the canoe but I don't think we can make it back to camp in this weather. Do you think we could wait it out in one of your cabins?"

Dorothy looked out the window at the falling snow, then over to the man on the cot. "Well," she said thoughtfully, "I guess you can stay right here in the main cabin."

"No, no," said Quint, "I don't want to intrude, especially when you have company."

Dorothy wearily drew herself up and said, "No, you'll stay here in the main cabin. I'm leaving. The US Forest Service float plane will be landing in about a half-hour. They'll help me bring my dad's body back to Ely. He died in his sleep last night."

If Quint had another hat to take off, he would have. As it was, he gripped his cap in both hands and rolled it over and over. He took another good look at the man laid out on the cot and this time saw the slackness of the facial muscles, the waxy skin, and the absolute stillness of the body. "Dorothy, I'm so sorry," he said kindly. "How can I help?"

It's funny how sometimes when you go looking for help you end up offering some instead.

●　●　●　●

10 • THE BEHAVIOR OF BULLETS

MY DAD, TO THIS DAY, still has the largest whitetail rack in the cabin. Back in 1946, he was hunting with some of his buddies east of Browerville, Minnesota, when he came across a massive white-tailed deer crossing the road. He was a fine, nine-point buck. Well, Dad's heart started pounding like it wanted out. He grabbed his rifle, kind of aimed, and fired. Unfortunately, on that first shot he only managed to take out both of the buck's hind legs. Once he was down, though, dad's second shot quickly found its mark, and he had the biggest trophy of his life. It was a beautiful mount.

After Dad shot-and-shot-again that first trophy, he had a long dry spell. Maybe the other deer got the word out? By the time I was 14, I was ready to join him on hunts. One sunny day, we were driving about a mile from our farm when we spotted a nice doe in the woods about 60 feet from the passenger side door; point-blank range as hunting deer goes. Dad told me to grab my gun and he pulled the car over.

I leveled my 12-gage slug gun on the deer's back. I wanted to hit the lungs, so I aimed a little high to compensate for bullet-drop. Bullet-drop is the vertical distance a bullet will fall while it also moves forward. The idea being, aim a little high and by the time the bullet gets there, it will have dropped a little and hit the bullseye. I pulled the trigger. BOOM! The gun kicked and then smoked a little, but the deer was safe from

53

me. She went bounding off into the woods, healthy as could be. Dad was not happy.

"Where'd you aim, Gary?" he asked, upset.

"Right level with the back," I said. I felt terrible for missing. I shot over the top of the deer.

"No, no—from this distance you've got to aim where you want to hit. There's no bullet drop on 60 feet," he said.

"Got it," I said, my eyes downcast. I felt so bad about missing that "gimme" deer. I decided I needed to do some target practicing at various distances.

I guess my heart was on my sleeve because Dad said, "Well son, don't worry about it. There's a lot of room around 'em."

Dad always saw more deer than any of us other hunters, but he shot less. About 20 years after his trophy shot, he and I were hunting together again. He spotted a deer, but it spooked and started running. When you're shooting at a running deer, you need to aim a little ahead of the animal, so the bullet and the target reach the same spot at the same time. It's called "leading." That's what my dad taught me, but he had a difficult time judging it for himself.

Maybe he just had a bad case of what is commonly known as "buck fever." As Dad spotted that small buck, his heart got pounding, his gun came up, and again he shot out the hind legs. Again, he had to walk up to it before finishing it off. Looking at the messy hind end, he rubbed the stubble of his chin thoughtfully and said, "You know Gary, I must not be leading 'em enough."

I chuckled a little and said, "Well Dad, don't worry about it. There's a lot of room around 'em." We smiled at each other.

● ● ● ●

11 • THE CHUTE

EAR FALLS, ONTARIO, CANADA IS about a 13-hour drive from Rochester, Minnesota. We drove an all-nighter to get to there because we wanted to save a vacation day. I had two weeks off per year from Rochester Datronics—one for family, and one for fishing and hunting—so there was no time to lose!

On this trip, Quint had his young son, Andy, join our hunting party. After work on Friday, we loaded the truck with hunting gear and topped it off with two canoes. With Quint and I taking turns at the wheel, we made the Ministry of Natural

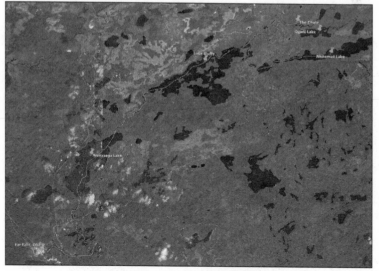

Canoe route from Ear Falls, ON, to The Chute.

Resources office in Ear Falls by 7:45 a.m. We walked into the office at 7:55 a.m. and found the agent sitting in his chair.

"Good morning," said Quint.

The MNR agent looked up from his desk, "Morning."

"We'd like to buy fishing and hunting licenses."

He gazed at Quint and languidly said, "We don't open 'til eight-o-clock."

Quint blinked. He looked pointedly at his watch that read 7:56 a.m. and then back to the agent.

The agent's lip curled, and he said, "They don't push me," and he visually dismissed us as he casually returned his attention back to the newspaper he was reading.

At eight-o-clock, precisely, we commenced with the business of buying fishing and hunting licenses that, for $101.00, would allow us to legally shoot nearly anything on a sidetrack. All we wanted was moose.

Ear Falls is the jump-off point for the Wenasaga River system and its several interconnected lakes. We made our way to the "Chute," about seven or eight hours upstream on the Wenasaga River. It's a small waterfall, about three or four feet high, that "chutes" along the river like a water slide. It's a beautiful spot with a very handy campsite right next to it. We could hunt the river upstream to Ogani Lake, or downstream to Whitemud Lake, Bluffy Lake, or back to Wenasaga Lake: it was all excellent moose country.

For 15 years we returned again and again to the Chute. The mid-'80s would bring heavy logging, a hunting season that didn't include the rut, and unaffordable permits, but in 1969, we loved it.

One year, Quint and I had made the trip with a couple friends. We'd been hunting for a few days when Quint and I decided to canoe our way up the Wenasaga River on a beautiful, clear evening. The other guys chose to stay behind at camp. I had the front seat. We had to portage to get around a 10-foot waterfall, but it wasn't too hard since we were traveling light at the time. I was carrying a Savage Model 99, lever action rifle, with 180-grain .300 Savage cartridges. We rounded a bend and all a sudden a huge cow moose stood up. I took aim, fired, and she dropped from a clean shot to the vitals. Just then, her calf stood up.

"Shoot the calf! Shoot the calf!" shouted Quint, a consummate meat hunter.

He didn't have to tell me twice. I dutifully obeyed and dropped the bull calf too.

"Wow!" I shouted, "Two of 'em! Wow!" I was elated! It was my first two-moose down.

We got to the work of skinning, gutting, and bagging, but before we'd even finished gutting one of them, night was on us. It took about three or four hours to get the meat into the canoe, even with the Coleman lanterns. When we finally boarded our small craft, we were both exhausted. It was pitch dark, and we still had a long way back to camp, including one long portage.

We loaded our canoe down with so much moose meat that the gunwale was a mere three inches above the water. We had to paddle very carefully and not tip the boat to one side or the other. We sat exactly in the middle and coordinated our movements so we didn't drop one side under water.

Quint said, "Part your hair in the middle!" and he was right, just one hair too many on one side could have tipped us.

Fortunately for us, the evening was perfectly still, without a ripple on the lake. Looking up, I could see the entire universe. There was no light pollution, no clouds, and the heavens were shining. As tired as I was, it was a wonderful kind of exhaustion. The kind when you know you got tired doing worthwhile things.

We'd been gone for quite some time and the guys back in camp decided they'd better come looking for us. We were in the middle of Rice Lake when we saw the lantern on their canoe. I slid my hand down the outside of our canoe and felt water only two knuckles down. I sure hoped that they didn't put up a lot of wake, or we'd be sunk. Their lantern light got brighter and brighter as they came closer and closer. I could make out the V-shape on the water behind their canoe and crossed my fingers.

"Slow down!" both Quint and I shouted, waving our arms in the up-and-down motion, universally known to mean *slow down*. It was probably a futile gesture, since they could no doubt only see our lantern, as we could only see theirs.

Fortunately, they slowed down. As the wake came upon us, it rose right to the top of the gunwale and hovered there, like water that rises higher than the edge of the glass but doesn't actually spill over. And then it was behind us. I breathed a sigh of relief.

Was I ever happy to see them. This meant that we'd have some help portaging our two moose, all our gear, and our canoe, around the waterfall. It was a tremendous amount of work after an already long day. We finally got back to camp at 1:00 a.m. I collapsed into my tent fully clothed. The last thing I remember thinking before sleep took me, was *I love my life*.

● ● ● ●

12 • TESTS AND TRIALS

IN 1971, 3M BOUGHT ROCHESTER DATRONICS. Unfortunately (fortunately?), they only bought the designs, machinery, and inventory. Not the employees. It turned out to be a bad summer to be out of work. The government cut back the NASA budget tremendously after the moon landing in 1969, and engineers became a dime a dozen. After four months, I finally landed a job with Berkley & Co., in Spirit Lake, Iowa, now called Pure Fishing. Other than my mechanical engineering degree, I think the only reason I got the job was that I liked to fish. At any rate, I landed the dream job of designing rods and reels. I would be the Chief Engineer for Berkley & Co. for the next seven years.

Berkley Bedell was the founder of Berkley & Co. He was quite the guy. He was a Democratic congressman who ran six times and held the office for 12 years. He started his career when he took $50 from his paper route income to build his first business. He used hair from his dog, Stubby, and feathers from the chickens in the back yard as the materials for tying flies, which he then sold to the local tackle shops and tourists. By the time he graduated from high school, he had employees. In 1945, after the war, he started Berkley & Co. Initially, he worked with cable-wire leaders (a length of line attached to the working end of your fishing line that you attach rigs and lures to). He then got into extruding Trilene nylon monofilament fishing line. In the '60s he moved into the rod and reel business. By the '70s he was exporting internationally. That's when I came in. I designed, developed, and tested rods and reels for Berkley. I travelled all over the place testing product. For a guy who's loved fishing all his life, I landed the big one!

You might think that a guy who goes fishing for a living might want to do something else on his vacations, but you'd be wrong. I kept going back to Lake Wenasaga, and other places, time and again. There's just something about getting out into the wilderness with some friends that keeps me coming back. I love the outdoors: when I'm in nature I feel close to God's creation. As much as I love the comradery of hunting with a group of good guys, I also like to go off on my own too. Some people feel energized by being around other people, but I feel more energized by space. I feel completely recharged after an afternoon of fishing alone, or by hiking through the woods with only the sound of my own footsteps for company. I also like the physicality of it. I enjoy pushing myself to my limits—seeing where my edges are. Working for Berkley & Co was both a joy and a challenge. It was great to get out onto the water and take a paycheck to outthink fish. I generally loved it, but there were a couple of occasions where I might have earned a bonus for going above and beyond.

One of my projects was to design saltwater surf reels. My boss, Paul Johnson, suggested that I go to the outer bank of North Carolina for the testing. I jumped on that opportunity like a twister on a trailer park.

We made our way to Cape Hatteras, North Carolina. Hatteras Island is one of the barrier islands that make up 110 miles of the Outer Banks that parallel the Eastern Seaboard. Ships traveling the Eastern Seaboard often sail too close to the islands, to their ultimate peril; thus bestowing the islands with the moniker Graveyard of the Atlantic.

Karl, one of our sales reps in North Carolina, set up a day of mackerel fishing with a woman named Harriett: Captain Harriett of Cape Hatteras. Karl and I boarded Harriett's 18-foot fishing boat early in the morning. As we walked down the dock, I felt confident in the shining white boat with its clean white bimini to protect us from sun and rain—not that there was any risk of rain on that beautiful sunny morning.

We motored south to Ocracoke Inlet, one of only three inlets along the Outer Banks, and were about mid-way through the channel when Karl said, "Gary, check this out," pointing into the water beside the boat.

I leaned over the side. Just under the surface, I caught a flash of light and a streak of movement before it disappeared. It reappeared a moment later. There's something about even looking at a shark that makes one feel a chill. Maybe it's a basic, primal instinct, like fearing snakes or sudden, loud noises. At any rate, they are fascinating to see and difficult to take your eyes off. Several sharks followed us through the channel before letting us pass, unmolested.

Once through the Ocracoke Inlet, we turned north and followed the coast back up to the outer side of Cape Hatteras. We would spend the day fishing the deeper, Atlantic water. A beautiful lighthouse stands tall there, with black and white stripes wrapping it like a barber's pole. Fishing was excellent, and we nearly filled our box with Spanish mackerel. Eventually, I became conscious of bobbing up and down more actively than we had been. Harriett said, "The wind is picking up, we should be getting back soon."

I turned my attention skyward, and although there was only blue with a few wisps of cloud, the ocean had lost its smoothness and had become quite choppy. We all reeled in and stowed our gear for the trip back.

It was a much rougher on the ride south to Ocracoke Inlet, with the waves hitting the boat broadside, picking us up several feet and dropping us into the troughs, picking us up, putting us down. Harriett seemed to have a good handle on it, though, maneuvering the little vessel such that no waves pushed us around too much. I guess you could say she wasn't a pushover.

I stood in the middle of the boat, holding onto the sturdy frame of the canvas cockpit cover, my feet firmly planted on the deck. It seemed to calm as we made the turn west to enter the inlet, putting our stern into the waves. Instead of rocking us side to side, the waves just pushed us forward. As we reached the middle of the channel, I happened to look back, and my eyes bugged out.

There was a 10-foot wave coming at us like an 18-wheeler bearing down on a tricycle! I ducked my head, held my breath, and hung onto that bimini for dear life!

"HOLD ON!" cried Harriett.

WHOOSH! Suddenly I was practically underwater as the wave crashed over the boat, then I was standing knee deep in it.

"ARE YOU GUYS OKAY?" she shouted to us.

"I'M GOOD!" I replied.

"YA, I'M OKAY!" replied Karl.

We were deep in a trough, and I could see another huge wave building behind us. I decided this would be a good time to put on a lifejacket. Fortunately, there just happened to be a few jackets floating freely in the foot of water sloshing around us. I grabbed one and put it on quickly, then handed Karl the other. Meanwhile, as the second wave built, Harriett opened the throttle and moved the boat into a position so that she surfed the boat along that wave and the next few huge waves, all the way through the channel! After that second wave, I crawled on all fours to the back of the boat, which was heaving, to pull the bilge plug and let the water out of the boat. Wave after wave we were hanging ten, surfing through the channel. Our lives hung on Harriett's experience and skill in handling that boat. She never let us down.

Just as suddenly as that first wave picked us up, the water suddenly calmed. We had made the starboard turn to north, back up the inside of Hatteras Island to Cape Hatteras. When I stood up from where I'd been clinging to the back of the boat, my knees were, in truth, shaking like a landed trout. I had not expected this trip to be one of my "sidetracks." I guess sometimes you look for a sidetrack, and other times you just get sidetracked! When I had two feet firmly planted back ashore, my knees still knocking, I said a quick prayer, thanking the Lord for a safe landing.

When we got back to the hotel, I opened my tackle box, which was wet; took out my camera bag, which was wet; removed my Zeiss-Icon Contaflex camera, which was wet; and removed the film canister, which was—you guessed it—wet. That was a lot of wet!

Later that night, I had dinner with Karl, who still had a pale green cast around his eyes. I told him about my film and said, "I guess I won't be showing pictures of this trip to the kids."

He smiled ruefully, "No, I guess not."

"You know," I added, "I can honestly tell Berkley that I *risked my life* to test our rods and reels." I thought a moment longer and said, "Think I can get a bonus?" Karl just shook his head at me. I grinned.

My next misadventure for Berkley & Co. came when they called on me to test the saltwater equipment on Albacore tuna. This time my boss, Paul, myself, and a few others, travelled to San Diego, California, where we boarded a 45-foot boat at midnight. Paul seemed somewhat reluctant to go after hearing about my last ocean-going excursion, but I was game—duty called. We had a six- or seven-hour run down the coast to Mexico.

That far out to sea, the waves were a good seven feet high. They weren't crashing over us, but they sure were picking us up and putting us down. We were rocking, rolling, pitching, and yawing. So was my stomach. I typically feel a little seasick on a boat if I don't have a decent breakfast, and this was no exception. Unfortunately, the only thing we had to eat on board was some greasy fried chicken. I can't say that's a good choice for anyone whose gills are already green.

Ignoring the nausea, or at least trying to, I dropped my line into the water and hoped an Albacore would hit, if for no reason but to take my mind off being sick. Usually, the thrill of catching a fish was such a rush that it would be all I was aware of. I'd be 100 percent in the zone. Not so much this time. I landed two good-sized, torpedo-like Albacore and decided that I absolutely had to eat something.

I made my way to the galley and grabbed a chicken leg that desperately needed an oil change. It was oozing grease. It's a testament to my hunger that I even took one bite, but one bite was all it took to send me staggering for the rail, churning for what seemed like an hour. I'd feed the fish, pause to get my breath, chum, breathe, chum, breathe . . . . Paul came over to me in-between bouts of vomiting.

"You okay?" he asked.

It was kind of a dumb question, given the circumstances, but I replied, "Oh yeah. Hey—do you think I can get a bonus *now?*" He just shook his head at me and walked away. I grinned. Then threw up again.

My test report to Berkley read: *The Trilene line exhibited good knot strength, low stretch, and is highly resistant to bodily fluids. It withstood the acidity of my churn exceedingly well.*

● ● ● ●

13 ● KILLING MOOSE AND DODGING BULLETS

BY NOW, QUINT AND I had been hunting the Wenasaga Lake area for several years. One fall, we went with our buddies, Skip and Tom. We decided to give ourselves a break from all the work of portaging canoes, gear, and meat around all the waterfalls. Instead, we would portage two canoes and some gear to the Chute, but have a floatplane deliver a 14-foot aluminum boat and its accompanying engine from Wenasaga Lake to Lake Ogani, relieving us of having to slog all that weight for the seven- to eight-hour trip. At the end of the week, we would have the plane fly out the aluminum boat, the engine, and all the meat back to Wenasaga Lake.

There was one seat available for someone to join the pilot when he picked up our gear from Wenasaga Lake, so Skip and Tom agreed to draw straws to see who would be the lucky co-pilot.

Whoever flew would not have to endure the hard work of loading all his gear and heading upstream for a brutish day of motoring and portaging. Instead, he would get to ride shotgun in a small plane over some beautiful country, and if he were lucky, he would even get to see game. So, it was with great anticipation that the four of us stood in a circle on the dock to see which guy would win.

Quint held out his fist holding two pieces of straw. The short straw had to portage.

"You go first," said Tom to Skip.

"Nuh-uh, you go first," said Skip.

Tom raised one eyebrow and responded by pulling one of the straws. He frowned and held it up for us to see, "Looks pretty short to me." We agreed, commiserating.

Then Skip slowly drew out the remaining, even shorter, straw.

"HAH!" shouted Tom, and he did a little victory dance there on the dock—much to Skip's chagrin.

Skip offered his hand to Tom and said, "Congratulations," but if Skip knew what was coming for Tom, he might have offered sympathy instead.

Tom helped us load the two canoes and saw us off. Quint and I in one canoe, Skip in the other, with the 14-foot aluminum sitting on the dock waiting for the plane to come and pick it up.

"See you around dusk!" called Tom as we shoved away from the dock.

"Have a safe flight!" shouted Quint.

"Thanks!" Tom waved as we pulled away.

I remember looking behind me and seeing Tom standing at the end of the dock with the aluminum boat, the engine, and a pile of gear behind him. The wind was coming up and it was just beginning to lightly rain. The plane would be there soon.

It would be a while before I heard about what happened to Tom, but from what I gathered, it went something like this: Not long after the canoes had dropped out of sight, Tom heard the distinctive drone of a floatplane approaching. He looked up to see its silhouette against the high, dense cloud. As it got closer he could see that it had a red stripe running along the sides, along the front of the wings, and around the nose by the propeller. The wind had come up quite a lot, along with the drizzle. The plane bucked its wings and waggled violently as it dropped into its approach. Tom watched helplessly as the little airplane got knocked around like a bad boxer, getting closer and closer to the water. He wanted to look away but couldn't.

The plane was just a few feet from touchdown when the wings suddenly tilted and skimmed the wave crests. At the same time, one pontoon scored the surface of the lake. Tom held his breath. Everything seemed to slow down. The plane blasted through the water in that position: one wingtip scudding across the top of the little waves, and one pontoon in the water, for what seemed like forever. Then, slowly, glacially, the wings leveled out. The second pontoon set down and kicked up even more spray, sending up a huge rooster-tail behind it. It skimmed along, slowed, and settled into the water as it taxied toward Tom, who was still holding that breath. Realizing he wasn't witnessing an aero-accident, his sense of time returned to normal speed, and he blew the stale air from his lungs.

The plane was a de Havilland Beaver, circa—well—it looked like something the Wright brothers might have flown, but it could have been a relic from WWII. The red stripes he'd seen earlier, he could now see were flaking and peeling. The windows were yellow with age. He could see that the aluminum pontoons were suffering from several areas where corrosion bubbles had formed. Despite the broken-down appearance of the vehicle, the pilot expertly maneuvered into position. As it gracefully glided alongside the dock, a man opened the pilot's door, stepped down onto the pontoon, and hopped onto the dock, where he secured the plane to a cleat with practiced ease.

The pilot looked to be in his forties. He was a wiry guy with hair nearly everywhere. It sprouted out his collar, his ears, and even his nose. He wore a Zappa style mustache but no beard. His ears stuck out like stop signs on a school bus. He stood and looked at the pile of gear, the boat, the engine, and with no small amount of sarcasm said, "Gee, is that all?"

"At least I didn't bring the piano," said Tom, walking forward to shake the man's hand. "Tom," he said as they shook.

"Artie," said the pilot, grinning.

"Good to know you," said Tom.

"Ahh . . . you say that now," said Artie with a wink. "So, 'sall this gettin' loaded up?"

"Yessir," said Tom. "They told us you can handle the boat alright, hope that's true."

"Oh sure, that's no problem. Here, get on that end." Artie and Tom hefted the 14-foot boat off the dock and wrangled on the pontoon and against the wing strut, and Artie began tying it down.

"Anything else I can do?" asked Tom.

"Sure. You can load the gear into the back if you'd like. Put it behind the cargo net," said Artie, and he turned back to tying the boat to the floatplane.

Tom made several trips back and forth with the gear. He had to climb onto the pontoon and up a ladder each time. After a while, all he had left to do was load the engine, and that was a two-person job. He waited on the dock, under the wing, to keep out of the drizzling rain, and watched Artie. He wondered if the guy had been a deckhand on a tugboat in an earlier career, or maybe an escape artist—judging by the way he was strapping the boat down. He'd started with rope, and now he was using duct tape. It wasn't long before Tom started shivering. How long was this going to take? He wanted to get on with it. He wanted to get to Ogani Lake and settle in. He wanted to get out of the rain and into the heated cockpit. Artie was taking forever to tie that boat down.

"Artie! What's taking so long?" he asked.

Artie smiled with big, white teeth and said, "If just one of these straps comes loose, we die."

"Check 'em again, Artie. Good man."

"Uh huh," said Artie with that toothy grin as he turned back to his work. He was reinforcing his knot work with duct tape.

Several minutes later, a dripping Artie finally stepped onto the dock to survey his work. "Hope that holds 'er."

Tom glanced at him, mildly concerned about his use of the word "hope."

"Let's get that engine strapped down inside and get going," said Artie.

The two men wrestled the 25-horsepower engine aboard, and Artie strapped it down using a couple of D-rings bolted to the floor, "That's got it. Let's go."

Tom climbed into the right-hand seat, did up his seatbelt, and donned a headset that would enable him to speak with Artie, as well as protect his hearing in the deafening cockpit noise. Tom, being an observant kind of guy, noticed that there were several holes in the dash where instruments once were.

"Hey, uh, Artie?" said Tom.

"Ya?"

"What's supposed to be in these holes?" Tom pointed to about five round gaps.

"Aw, nuthin'. Don't worry about it, we just need the gas gage," said Artie, tapping a gage that showed about two-thirds full.

"How about a compass?" Tom asked dubiously.

"Naw. I've been flying around here since Jesus wore short pants. I know how to get to Ogani," said Artie. Tom nodded, almost convinced, but he still wondered about a black box.

Artie turned his attention to the knobs and levers of the plane, but the old machine didn't seem to be much interested in what Artie wanted or didn't want. She just groaned and coughed, sputtered, and spat. Artie mumbled something under his breath and continued in his attempt to coax life into the little bird. The plane continued to ignore him. Finally, losing patience, Artie pounded on the yoke and shouted, "COME ON, YOU OLD WHORE!"

To which, the plane exploded into a roar of life, propeller spinning merrily.

Artie quickly slipped the lines from the dock, and they were soon taxying out into the lake—which, fortunately, was very long. The waves were still a bit choppy on the water, so the ride to the aerodrome was bumpy. Once they got far enough out and pointed into the wind, Artie did a quick check of a few things and then pushed the yoke forward. The plane roared even louder, if that were possible, and dug in for takeoff. The plane moved forward, but on a quick walk instead of a run. It didn't seem like she'd get enough speed to lift off.

Through the headset, Tom could hear Artie saying, "Come on . . . come on . . ." as they bumped across the water. "It's the boat . . ." he said.

"What about the boat?" asked Tom, eyes huge.

"The boat's causing some drag," said Artie, his hairy knuckles turning white as they gripped the yoke.

The opposite shore was getting closer and closer. Tom could just make out individual reeds swaying in the water.

The plane bounced off a particularly sharp wave, and they were suddenly airborne. Tom watched the lake fall away. He turned his attention to the horizon, which all of a sudden tilted! Then it tilted the other way! Then the rear of the plane bucked like a wild pony, and Tom's breakfast got very light in his stomach. Despite the rocky ride, they were climbing. Once they reached about 2,000 feet, they leveled off. The air at that altitude was less turbulent, and Tom's death-grip on the door handle eased off. About 10 minutes into the flight, the clouds thinned out, and the rain stopped. From that height, they had a bird's-eye-view of the whole forest, with its pristine lakes and winding rivers and creeks. It was truly majestic.

"Nice view, eh?" said Artie.

Tom nodded and said, "Not bad!"

The rest of the flight went smoothly. Tom relaxed into his seat and enjoyed the ride. After some time, they dropped altitude, and Ogani Lake came into view. Artie pointed it out to Tom, but Tom had already figured it out for himself. As they came in for their approach, Tom got thinking about the last, very dodgy, landing he saw Artie make, and he became conscious of his own mortality once again. *It's not the fall that'll kill you, it's the landing,* he thought to himself. Fortunately, there was virtually no wind and no rain, so the landing was smoother than a politician's promise.

There being no docks on the lake, Artie slipped over to the shore and lightly beached the plane. He and Tom climbed onto the pontoons and untaped/untied the aluminum boat. Together, they wrestled the engine out of the fuselage and hooked it onto the stern of the boat. Then, Artie passed the remaining gear down to Tom, who piled it all on the little beach. The two shook hands and Artie said, "See you in a week!"

Tom helped Artie shove the plane back into the lake. He stood on shore but was ready to jump into the boat just in case he had to retrieve the plane if it didn't start. The last he saw of Artie that day was through the cockpit window where he was pounding on the yoke of the little plane, shouting, and calling her bad names, just before the engine caught and the propeller began to spin merrily. If ever there was a dysfunctional relationship . . . .

It was nearly dark by the time Quint, Skip, and I approached the Chute. The sky was that deep, electric blue that it gets just after the sun's gone down, with a thin line of orange silhouetting the trees. There was the glow of Tom's campfire against the black velvet of his camp. We motored right up to the beach and cut the engines. Tom was there, rested, and ready to help us with the canoes and gear.

"How was the trip?" he asked.

"Long," I replied, weary from eight hours of portaging canoes and gear. "But it still beats a day at the office! How was your flight?"

Tom thought about that for a moment and replied, "I guess it had its ups and downs." Later, over the fire with a cup of tea, Tom told us all about his adventures with Artie. "Maybe next week I'll leave the long straw for Skip."

As always, the week of fishing and hunting renewed my spirit and rejuvenated my energy. There's nothing quite like fly fishing a waterfall alone. I find it so relaxing to immerse myself in the task of baiting a hook or finding my footing along river rocks. The musical rhythm of casting a line out and back, out and back, out and back, is somehow healing. Then, the challenge of tracking big game through dense forest, and the sense of conquest when I shoot one, affects me in much the same way that I imagine it has affected hunters throughout time: I feel exhilarated, victorious, but also humbled and grateful. The comradery of my friends is icing on the cake.

By the end of the week, we had a good-sized moose and our limit of fish swimming around our makeshift live well. On the appointed day of departure, we awoke to heavy fog and mist, with a cloud ceiling lower than the bottom button on a turtle's vest. The chances of seeing a floatplane that day weren't looking good, but we still hoped.

"You want to draw straws on who gets to go by air?" Skip asked Tom.

"Uh—no. It's all yours, buddy," said Tom, grinning.

Skip couldn't be sure who was getting the better deal, but

since Tom had already done one flight, it seemed to make sense that he go. "Okay," he nodded dubiously.

Shortly after breakfast, we filleted our limit of walleyes and broke camp. Our plan was to have Skip fly back with the aluminum boat and the meat, while the remaining three of us took the two canoes back down to Wenasaga Lake. Now, as we stared glumly at the darkening clouds that seemed to be dropping instead of burning off, we got talking about plan-B.

Skip said, "You guys can take the canoes, and I'll stay behind with the aluminum and wait for the plane."

"No way," I shot back at once. "If I let you do that, and the plane can't make it and leaves you stranded here, your wife would skin me alive."

Skip laughed but said, "Yeah, I guess she would."

"We don't leave any man behind," said Quint. We all nodded in agreement.

"So," said Tom, "Do we re-pitch camp and all stay another day? Or, do we put the meat in one of the canoes and tow it behind the aluminum? Gary and Quint can take the aluminum and Skip and I can take the rest of the gear in the canoe. Try to make Wenasaga before dark?"

Skip nodded slowly, pondering the options. "If we're gonna try for the lake, we've got to leave now."

We all stood on the beach, looking at the calm water and dark sky. Tom skipped a flat stone, and we watched it bounce two, three, four times. The ripples from the rock joined the ripples from the few raindrops that had just started to fall.

"I don't think we're gonna see that plane today," said Tom. We all looked up at the low ceiling, impossible for a plane without instruments to navigate. "Besides, we've all got to make it back to work on Monday."

"I say we go now," I said.

Quint nodded, "I second that."

Everyone else agreed, and we went to work loading the boats.

We all filled one of the canoes to the brim with moose meat and fish. Then Tom and Skip loaded the second canoe with gear. Quint and I loaded up the aluminum with the remaining gear and arranged a bridle to tow the meat-canoe behind us. All three boats were at maximum capacity. There was a feeling of urgency and trepidation as we shoved off the pebbly beach.

As we motored our way down the river, a breeze began to blow. The clouds dropped even more. If they dropped much further, they'd be fog. It was cold, and I could smell snow.

The breeze freshened, and by the time we made it to the aptly named Bluffy Lake, there were two-foot waves breaking and swamping the canoes. I looked over at Tom and Skip's canoe and saw that Skip was bailing out water. This worried me. I turned to look at the canoe we were towing behind us, riding low with its heavy load. As I watched, a good-sized wave hit it square on the beam, causing it to tip sideways and scoop up a large amount of lake water. Now it tilted seriously, and we were in danger of losing all the moose meat and gear.

Quint was on the tiller, so I shouted to him, "There!" I pointed to a rocky island nearby, "Let's get it over to that island before we lose everything!"

Quint steered us over to the island, but before we got there, all we could effectively do was watch the canoe behind us tilt increasingly sideways with each wave. Then, we watched as an entire hind quarter of moose-meat slipped out of the canoe and down to Davey Jones's locker, never to be seen by human eyes again.

Fortunately, a moose is a very large animal. It dresses out at about 400 pounds, so the loss of the hind quarter hardly left us empty handed, but the rest of the precious cargo was about to go the same way. I was not *really* thinking about swimming for it when we suddenly bumped against the rock island.

Quint reached behind him to grab the tow-rope and positioned the canoe between a couple of rocks that would support it. We maneuvered our own boat so we were able to disembark. Now we were able to pull the canoe up on shore a bit. We worked quickly to unload all the cargo and then tip the canoe upside down to drain the water. Tom and Skip stayed in their canoe, bailing water.

We reloaded the meat back into the canoe and boarded the aluminum boat again. We sat low in the water with our heavy load, but the canoe rode a little higher now that it had been emptied of water and a hind quarter of moose. The snow I'd been smelling finally materialized and the air was all flurries. The wind was whipping our wet clothes against us. I couldn't feel a single finger or toe by the time we finally shoved off. Quint slouched as low as he could get in the boat and still steer. I looked over at the other canoe and saw Tom all hunkered down as small as he could get. Skip looked like a lump of misery, hunched over in the boat with his cap low and hands stuck in his armpits.

We were half-way across the lake when I had a thought.

"Hey Quint! Have you seen the game seal?" A game seal is a metal tag that you attach to your kill and which can't be unattached. By law, you must keep it on the animal while it's transported. Without it, you can get fined big-time.

"Aww . . ." Quint said, "I put it on the hind quarter that sank!"

We sat there for a moment, just looking at one another. Then I shrugged and said, "Well there's nothing we can do about it now."

On our final portage, the snow began to swarm like angry bees. After several trips, back and forth to move both canoes, the boat, our gear, and the meat, there were six inches of snow on the ground.

"Well guys," said Skip, "what do you think about m-making camp here for the night?"

He had a point. It was getting late, but I said, "I don't know, I think we should just press on."

"How much further do we have to go?" asked Tom.

"About three miles of river and another eight on Wenasaga Lake," I said.

Quint said, "Yeah, I think I'd rather keep going. I don't want to have to cut all the poles and stakes to get the tent up again."

Quint had a tent that must have been designed by a one-eyed simpleton before they invented aluminum or fibreglass. He actually had to use a hatchet to cut up sticks to use as pegs and poles. "Might be time for a new tent," I said.

"Don't I know it?" he muttered.

Tom agreed, and Skip reluctantly went along, so we got back into the boats and pushed off. In hindsight, we probably should have listened to Skip. The rest of the trip down the river was uneventful, but full darkness had fallen by the time we reached Wenasaga Lake. The snow was now coming down like a flock of buckshot ducks, and the wind was howling. The waves on the lake kept getting bigger and the wind caught the tips of the waves and sprayed us with them. It wasn't fully dangerous yet, but it was clearly time to abandon plan-B and seek shelter.

"Look!" shouted Quint over the noise of the wind and engine, "See the light?" A dim light was just visible on the horizon, about three miles away.

"Yeah!" I shouted back, "Let's go!" I knew there was a lodge with a few hunting cabins surrounding it in that area.

"Go to the lee of that island," shouted Skip from the canoe, pointing.

"Good idea!" Quint steered us to where the waves were smaller, and the wind was weaker. We kept a close eye on the light in the distance and our spirits grew with its intensity. As we approached, we spotted the dock and made a beeline for it. The waves still tossed us around and were wet to the bone.

As we neared the dock, I leaned out to grab a cleat and pulled the aluminum boat alongside. Stiff and cold, Quint and I crawled out of the boat and stood wobbly as we tried to work blood back into our hands and feet. Tom and Skip had pulled alongside in their canoe, but Skip was so cold and weak that he wasn't able to get out of the canoe by himself. The three of us pitched in to help Skip out; he was in the early stages of hypothermia and shaking like a Baptist on a barstool.

We secured the meat-canoe while Tom tied up behind it. With Quint on one side and me on the other, we managed to walk Skip to the light that had guided us in. It belonged to a group of hunters who had rented one of the little cabins on the property. We banged on the door and a bearded man opened it.

"Hello? Hey! Wow, ya, come on in," the guy saw at once that we had a situation on our hands and opened the door wide. Closing it behind us, he introduced himself. "I'm Gerald, this is John, and that's Bruce," he said.

We introduced ourselves and got Skip sitting down near the cozy wood stove while Quint rummaged through Skip's pack for some dry clothes. Gerald had some sweet, warm tea in Skip's hands and a blanket around him before Tom even had his boots off. Once the situation looked under control, I said to Quint, "I'm going to go back to the canoes. They're getting knocked around pretty good and I'm worried."

"Good idea, do you want a hand?" Quint asked. Tom and Skip huddled close to the fire; they both looked frozen. I'd warmed up a little with the effort of tying up the boats and getting Skip indoors. I felt okay—well, as okay as possible in the circumstances.

"No," I said, "you stay here and warm up, I won't be long."

I returned to the dock to see our boats bashing into the little dock and taking on water with every wave that came along. It's a good thing I went back when I did because they were all about to sink. I bent to untie and move them when I heard a shout.

"Hey!" I looked up to see a white-bearded guy coming down the ramp toward me on the dock. He looked angry. And big. He was big. "This is a private dock!" he shouted. Even from that distance I could see the veins bulging in his neck.

Alarmed, I quickly rose from where I crouched beside a cleat, untying the boat. I took a step back before remembering that I was on a dock. Big angry guy on one side of me, short dock on the other.

"Yes, yes, I know, but—" I started.

"You can't tie up here without permission!" the man chastised.

"I realize, yes," I said.

"You need to take your canoes and move along," he said.

"Well, no. I can't do that. We've had some trouble," I said.

"What kind of trouble?" he asked suspiciously.

"My three buddies and I got caught out on the lake when the wind and snow came up. One of the canoes got swamped and dumped some of our meat," I indicated the tow-canoe with the bags of meat in it, half covered in water. "My one friend is hypothermic."

The big man asked, "Where is he now?"

"We followed that light to shore," I pointed at the light of the nearby cabin. "We knocked on the door and he's being taken care of by the guys there."

"Okay, that's good," he nodded suspiciously at the canoes. "How long do you plan on staying?"

"Just until our friend warms up. I have to get to the landing to get my truck and trailer," I said.

"Well . . . alright," he reluctantly agreed. "Those aren't going to make it long tied up there, though, you'd better get them moved."

He watched me, arms crossed and scowling, as I bailed each of the boats—by myself—and pulled them around to the lee of the docks and closer to shore where they were protected from the bashing waves—by myself. I made sure the cargo was still secure. I was annoyed that the guy just stood there watching me work without offering any help, but I figured I'd make the best out of the situation. I put my hand out, "I'm Gary."

"Dave. I'm the owner here," he said as he shook my hand. Now that he understood that I wasn't there to freeload off him, he seemed to relax a scintilla—but only *one* scintilla.

"You know, I have another small problem," I said. Dave kind of huffed like I was just one great problem for him, but I pushed on and explained to him about how we lost the game seal. "I wonder if I can use your phone to call the game warden and explain the situation. I think it's better to talk to him now, before getting caught without it."

"Yup, I guess that's a good idea. Come on up to the lodge," Dave said grudgingly. It was a beautiful, large, post-and-beam building. Dave directed me to the telephone and phone book, and I started dialing. And dialing. And dialing. Where is a game warden when you needed one? Eventually I gave up on it. Let the chips fall where they may.

I thanked Dave, picked up my backpack, and returned to the small hunting cabin. Gerald opened the door to me and I could see that the color had returned to Skip's face, although he still looked somewhat shaken.

"Gary, you're not going to believe these cookies!" said Quint, handing me the best chocolate chip cookie I've ever eaten in my life (sorry Ginny—it was the circumstances). Gerald gave me a strong, hot cup of coffee, and I finally sank into a chair, done.

But not done. After the coffee and the cookie, I rose to change into dry clothes. We had to keep moving or we weren't going to make it home in time for work on Monday. The three hunters were very accommodating, and Bruce agreed to drive Tom and me to the landing at Ear Falls so we could pick up my truck and trailer. We drove from the Ear Falls' landing back to the lodge where we all loaded up all our gear, game, and boats, and hit the road.

By two o'clock in the morning, we made the game check, which was about half-way to the US border. It turns out that's not a bad time of day to hit a game check, especially with a missing game seal. We had to wake up the attendant. He blearily found and handed over papers that would allow us to export the moose back to the States. We filled those out and then he said, "I just have to attach the export license to your game seal.

That'll be a neat trick, I thought to myself, picturing the guy in scuba gear at the bottom of Bluffy Lake, searching for that hind quarter of moose. "Okay, let me go find it," I said.

I climbed into the pitch-black trailer and rummaged around for the right length of time, then called out, "Found it!"

The sleepy attendant handed me the tag without wanting to see the game seal for himself. I took the export license from him and "attached" it.

"Thanks," I said as I climbed back out of the trailer.

"No problem," said the attendant. "You guys have a safe trip home."

We all thanked the attendant and watched as he walked

back into the building. Quint spoke for all of us when he said, "Bullet dodged."

Note to self: sometimes, when you can't seem to catch a break, it pays to make one for yourself.

● ● ● ●

Securing a canoe to a float plane.

14 • FINDING MY EDGES

ANOTHER YEAR, MY BROTHER, DON, me, and four others made camp at the Chute on the Wenasaga River. It was late October and the temperatures were reaching an unheard of, balmy 70°F. Don and I were in the canoe going up Rice Lake early one morning in search of moose. The ground fog, albeit beautiful in the dawn light, obscured the shoreline, making it tough to spot game. Don sat in the front end of the canoe this time. We'd take turns in that seat because it was the easiest place to shoot from. Something near shore caught my eye, just a glint of light that didn't fit.

"Don," I whispered.

He turned to me.

"Just there," I pointed to where I'd seen the light, maneuvering the canoe closer. "Get ready, I think something's there."

Don raised his gun to the ready.

Sure enough, there was a great big bull moose standing proud, chewing his cud. We got to within 90 feet, when the moose suddenly turned sideways in alarm. Don fired. He caught the animal's hip. It staggered and then took off into the brush.

Frustrated, Don turned to me and said, "You finish him off, Gary," and handed me his gun.

"Yup," I said as I beached the canoe, grabbed his gun, and launched myself onto shore in practically one motion.

Following the blood trail, I tracked the bull into the woods about a third of a mile. I could hear it wheezing occasionally, and I took a couple of shots at it through the thick brush, but I could never get a clean shot. Finally, I got a lung-shot with the last round in the rifle. In slow motion, the bull dropped to his knees and tipped over. It was bizarre how slowly that happened.

When the body was lying still on the ground, I cautiously approached with my hunting knife, ready to strike. My heart was pounding, not only because of the chase, but because I was approaching a *hopefully*-dead thousand-or-more-pound animal, with no more bullets and only a knife as a weapon. I reminded myself, *if you're not living on the edge you are taking up too much room.*

At that moment, no one could accuse me of taking up too much room.

The moose was dead as dead, and I breathed again.

The real work started with hauling the beast back to camp. It took 45 minutes with a chainsaw and hatchets just to make a reasonably decent trail from the fallen animal back to the canoe. We made many trips back and forth, hauling the moose out sections at a time. It was indeed a keeper, with a 49.5 inch rack and somewhere in the neighbourhood of 1000 pounds! It was starting to heat up as the day wore on. There was a small stream by the trail we'd carved out, and I stopped to sip from it every time I passed. It was going to take us all day to get that moose back to camp.

"Hey Gary," puffed Don as he walked ahead of me loaded down with meat.

"Yuh?" I grunted back. I was struggling with my own load.

"Do you remember Dad always saying, 'That Gunner sure are strong!' in his funny Swedish accent?"

"Hah! Yeah, I do, but I never understood why he got such a kick out of it. What was the story?"

"Well you know Grandpa Louis was adopted by a family that had emigrated from Sweden, right?" asked Don.

"Yeah."

"Gunner was one of the biological kids from that family, so he was Grandpa's brother."

"Okay, I knew that," I said.

"Yeah, so Gunner was this really big guy who could carry anything, and their dad would always say in a really thick Swedish accent," at this point Don adopted the accent and said, 'That Gunner sure are strong!'"

I chuckled a bit at that. Don was seven years older than me, so he tended to have a different set of memories.

Don went on. He was breathing hard as we walked but he still managed to talk. "HAH! I remember Dad telling me a story about Gunner. He said they used to hunt together a lot, back in the day. They'd have to travel 100 miles to the north, though. Back then, there were no deer where we lived because so little of the land was cleared. The deer would eventually populate the area as more and more farmers cleared the land, but back in their day, a hunting trip was a big deal. Gunner and Dad would get so excited, they'd stay awake all night long."

We reached the canoe and piled our meat into it, stretched our backs, then returned for more.

"So anyways," Don continued, "I remember Dad telling me about a time when they had travelled to Park Rapids and sat up drinking coffee all night in a cheap hotel. The next day—it was winter—they went out and shot a doe. They had to go out on a frozen lake, about three inches of ice, to get it. Gunner grabbed it by the hoof and began to drag it back to where they came from. Dad saw this and says to Gunner, 'Gunner, why don't you grab it by the head? You won't be dragging against the hair and it will go a lot easier.' Well—hah!—I guess Gunner—hah!—Gunner looked at Dad and then behind him at the doe, and he says, 'Then I'd get farther from the car!'"

"Hah!" I laughed. Don started laughing, too. In fact, he started snorting with laughter. Of course, that made me laugh even harder. Don had to stop walking because he was laughing so hard. We cracked up for a while, wiped tears from our eyes, took another drink from the stream, and kept on working.

We made it to camp at dusk. I'd never been that exhausted in my life. It was all I could do to get my body out of the canoe and over to a bush, where I promptly launched everything I'd eaten and drank that day. I was so exhausted that all I could do was crawl into my tent and collapse. The next morning, I woke to find that my feet were still sticking out the tent flap, my boots still on. I definitely pushed myself to my personal limits and found some more edges.

That was a memorable trip, not just because I pushed past the bounds of my physical abilities and brought home a monster-moose, but because a couple of the other guys in our hunting party, Lloyd and his son Randy, brought down the biggest moose of the year. To give perspective, the largest moose ever shot in that province had a 66-inch rack, and they brought down a bull with a 61.5-inch rack. They had an easier time getting their moose back to camp, however, because they were fortunate enough to shoot it close to the water.

The third pair of guys in our party could have bagged a third big bull that same day, but they messed up. I guess the guy in the back of the canoe got a little excited when they spotted the bull, because he wasn't looking where he was steering and put them right into some bushes. Of course, the guy in front couldn't see where to shoot, and the moose escaped. That senior moment cost us a hat trick on trophy bulls in one day. Nevertheless, it was a great trip; very satisfying in many respects.

● ● ● ●

15 • COMING OF AGE

BY 1977, QUINT AND I were both taking our sons, Andy and Troy, hunting with us. We made the trip back to Ontario, to the Wenasaga Lake area again, along with my brother, Don, and our friend, Harvey. I knew Harvey from Rochester and we became pretty good friends. I admired his energy and the way he could MacGyver nearly anything. When we first arrived at camp, Don lost his pipe, so Harvey just made him a new one with two half-moon shaped pieces of wood that he then duct-taped together. It might not have been the most elegant pipe ever created, but it worked for the rest of the week. When we broke camp, we found Don's original pipe under the ground tarp. I believe that anyone can accomplish anything with a roll of duct tape and a MacGyver attitude.

One day, Troy and I made a run downstream on the Wena-saga River, but never saw any moose at all. We got back to the Chute by dusk, but Quint and Andy weren't back from their run yet. I cooked up some dinner for Troy and me, but by the time I'd finished washing and drying the dishes, Quint and Andy still hadn't shown up. A cup of tea for me, a cup of cocoa for Troy. After a couple of hours, Troy asked, "What do you think could have happened to them?"

"They probably bagged a moose and it's just taking a while to get it back to camp," I said reasonably.

"Or they got eaten by a bear," said Troy.

I looked sideways at my nine-year-old and replied, "Or they bagged two moose and it's taking a while to get back to camp."

"Or they drown in the lake," said Troy.

"You want to go look for them?" I asked.

"Probably should," said Troy.

"Let's go," I said.

We loaded up the canoe with what provisions we thought we might need: lantern, flashlight, first aid kit, drinking water, and so on. We dropped the canoe in above the Chute and started across the two-mile-long Ogani Lake. I was running the engine and Troy was signalling everywhere with a heavy-duty flashlight. No signals came back. About half-way across the lake, a west wind began to pick up behind us and push our empty canoe across the choppy water at a gallop. I thought that if the wind pushed us like that, it would be nearly impossible for Quint and Andy to make any headway against it with their canoe weighed down with moose meat. The waves were getting bigger and bigger and the wind was starting to howl. Should I turn back with Troy? Should I keep searching for our friends?

No sooner had those worrisome questions occurred to me, then we saw a six-foot flash of gunfire explode some distance ahead of us. There they were! I powered over to where we'd seen the flash.

Sure enough, their canoe was sitting low in the water with several hundred pounds of moose meat. Both Quint and Andy looked tired, but healthy. Andy's eyes were the size of a hoot owl's in the night. Relieved to have found them, Troy and I took some of the weight from their boat to ours, and followed them as they slowly, but steadily, plowed their way through the wind and waves back to camp.

Once we had unloaded both canoes and settled, I asked Quint, "Why did you fire your gun? What happened to your flashlight?"

He looked a bit sheepish: "We forgot the flashlights."

"So, you saw our signal and fired, hoping we'd see the flash?" I asked.

"Actually, I thought you'd hear the shot. I didn't occur to me that it would be the muzzle flash that caught your attention," he said.

"No, I didn't hear a thing over the wind. I just happened to see the flash," I said. "Weren't you worried about the recoil causing the canoe to tip over?"

"Actually, yes. I figured that if I put the gun to my shoulder and fired, we'd go over. We were already so deep in the water with the load of meat. So, I put the butt of the rifle against the bottom of the canoe and fired straight up," said Quint.

"That worked," I said.

"Sure did," Quint said with a smile.

Later that week, Troy and I jumped into the canoe, heading for Whitemud Lake early in the morning. It was bitterly cold, and we were busting through a thin layer of ice part of the time. By about 8:00, Troy had enough, so we stopped to build a fire. It didn't take very long to heat up our hands and get back into the canoe. We were across to the other side of the lake when Troy suddenly pointed.

"Dad," he said in a stage whisper. "Look!"

There on the lake bank were two moose: a cow and a bull. I quickly raised my gun and shot twice. The cow cooperated nicely and dropped right there, but the bull took off running. I had shot him, so I knew he would run out of steam eventually but the further he ran, the further we'd have to haul the meat. We beached the canoe. I jumped out and started tracking. Fortunately, I didn't have to go far. About 100 feet from shore there was a pothole filled with water. The bull had run directly into it, and all that was showing was his nose and one horn. It wasn't much of a tracking job after all, but it would be a chore to get that moose out of the pit. This was a job for the come-a-long.

When hunting, I bring as little gear as possible, but there's still a lot of stuff. It's hard work packing and unpacking, especially when portaging, but I've found that the extra work usually pays off. On this trip, like most of my trips, I had a small come-a-long. That's a hand operated, one-and-a-half-ton winch with a ratchet used to pull things. One hook of the come-a-long attaches to line that wraps around an immovable object, in this case a tree; a second, "free" hook attaches to the movable object, in this case a moose stuck in a pit of muddy water. You just crank a lever on the come-a-long and the moveable line wraps around a small drum, pulling the moose out. For situations like this, it's the handiest tool ever, but you do need to use it with a little caution.

Once I was winching a moose out of another awkward place, about 150 feet from shore, and I anchored the fixed end to a tree. It was about 13 inches around and I tied onto it three feet from the ground. It seemed solid enough. Except it wasn't. I started cranking away on the winch and soon heard a sharp CRACK that sent me jumping back. The pressure of the rope broke the tree! It split, jerked, and then fell into the water. Ever since then I'm extremely careful about where I anchor a come-a-long: always check the strength of the tree, always place the rope or chain as low as possible, take nothing for granted.

Another time, my friend Jim had been hunting alone and bagged a moose. He got it into the river and managed to float it downstream, but he got it a little too close to some waterfalls. I'm not sure how long he'd been there, but a couple of us happened to be motoring upstream and looked up at the waterfall only to see half a moose hanging over the edge! We beached the canoe and ran to help him. He had the moose tied off to a tree, but he couldn't budge it an inch off the falls. I used the come-a-long and winched the huge animal onto a big rock. It's remarkable how many times I've winched moose in my lifetime.

Anyway, on this occasion with Troy, everything went smoothly. The tree held, and the bull came out of the mud pit without a hitch. Troy and I had our first load of moose in the canoe and we were back at camp by 11:00 a.m., just in time for lunch. By dinner we had all the meat at camp. Go team!

Troy, has always liked fishing and hunting. When he was young, I had to practically lock him in his room before I left on a trip without him. I'm surprised he never popped out of a trunk or a cooler after I got to a destination. However, I suppose every kid wants to be a grownup before his time, and I was no exception.

I remember when I was barely old enough to go to school, my preference was to work with the men during thrashing season and fill the silo. My mother, however, had other ideas. For some crazy reason, *way* beyond my understanding, she thought I should attend school instead of filling the silo. I simply could not understand that kind of thinking and refused to accept it. So one morning when my uncle Elmer tried to drop me off at school, when all the men were back on the farm filling the silo, I flat-out refused to go. I grabbed a hold of the car door's handle and wouldn't let go. The teacher came out of the school house and got a hold of me and pretty much had to pin me to keep me from crawling back into the car. She was a lot bigger than me, so she won. Why-oh-why couldn't they all recognize how much they needed me to help fill that silo? Grownups could be . . . well . . . dumb sometimes.

It would be a long time before I could call myself a man, but I suppose I did go through my fair share of rights-of-passage. One of those was trying a cigarette.

Frankie and Gary were a couple of grades older than me, and they decided that it was time we all try smoking. Frankie stole some smokes from his dad, and the next day, the three of us snuck out to the boys' outdoor toilet. Frankie handed me one and I lit it up and took a couple of puffs. I waited for something to happen. Something should have happened. *What's the point in smoking if nothing happens?* I wondered. I waited and waited but, in the end, nothing ever happened. I never got dizzy or sick or anything, like you hear other people say. I just thought it tasted bad and that it wasn't very smart or fun. Unimpressed, I threw the butt down the outhouse hole and went back to class.

That should have been the end of it, but I guess I carried the smell of the smoke on my clothes because the girls caught one whiff of me and, quicker than stink, the teacher knew all about it. All three of us got pulled into the teacher's office, but Frankie and Gary got in a lot more trouble than I did. Being older, I guess she felt that they should have known better than me. We were all suspended from recess, meaning that we wouldn't be allowed to go outside to play between classes; but they got a

My country school room. I'm in the fourth row from the left, four down. My aunt, Donna, is the teacher at the back of the room.

week, while I only got three days. No buzz, no nicotine high, and three days of punishment to show for it.

When I was about 13 years old, my uncle Tilford dropped by the farm. Tilford ran a gas station and was the mechanic and welder in the thriving metropolis of Rose City, Minnesota: population about 22. It's the town that time forgot. The locals mostly ran small farms and tended toward . . . let's call it "fiscal responsibility." They'd rarely put more than a buck of gas into their vehicles, and they'd get an oil check and their windshields washed for that same buck. Uncle Tilford told me a story once about this one farmer, Milo. He'd come by the shop and ask Tilford for the used oil he'd drained from other vehicles' oil changes. That was fine by Tilford; he'd just have to dispose of it anyway. Milo would pour it into his truck and when he got to the bottom of the container, where all the sludge and bits were, he'd just keep on pouring.

"That sludge isn't good for your engine, you know," Tilford advised Milo.

To which Milo replied, "Naw. It's the sludge that really makes her puuurrr." Well that just cracked Tilford up.

Anyhow, Tilford dropped by the farm that day, not for Dad but for me.

"Gary, you want to come duck hunting with me and Royal?" he asked. Royal was a good buddy of his.

"I sure do!" I replied. *Are you kidding?* I thought. This would be my very first real duck hunting trip.

"Well, all right then," said Tilford, "Go see if you can borrow your dad's gun and let's go. We're going to pick up Ken, too." Ken was a buddy of mine.

I ran to get the gun and the eagerly hopped into the back seat of Tilford's car. We picked up Ken along the way. Why Tilford would want to bring along a couple of kids who'd never shot into the sky, much less hit a bird, I'll never know, but I was happy to go along.

Ken and I had each borrowed our dads' single-shot 12-gage shotguns and the four of us headed for Ken's dad's slough. It was a fine, bluebird day. The sun was shining and there wasn't a cloud in the sky. There weren't any ducks either. We knelt in the duck blind for a quite a while before Til and Royal decided to leave us put and head out for a different slough.

As Ken and I sat in the duck blind, we didn't fidget or talk. I wondered about the duck's eyesight and worried that the reason they weren't flying was because Ken and I weren't wearing camouflage; but at that time, you couldn't buy it in stores, and even if you could, we couldn't have afforded it. We just pushed further into the long grass and hoped for the best. Eventually, our patience paid off. I spotted a lone drake mallard soaring high overhead. Quick as I could, I pulled up on it and BOOM! To my utter surprise, it dropped like a meteor.

I'd never seen such a beautiful duck. Never.

Not much later, Tilford and Royal returned. I guess they heard the shot and wanted to find out what we got. I stood proudly with my catch and privately noted that they were coming back empty-handed. They were full of sour grapes when they saw that I had such a beautiful bird and they only had skunk. "Beginner's luck," they said. I didn't mind; I knew what I had.

At the end of the day, Uncle Til divided the ducks. To my chagrin, he kept the drake mallard for himself and gave me a couple of green-wing teal. It would have been wonderful to have shown that drake to my dad. Although I felt dismayed at first when I saw what Til had done, it didn't take but a few moments to let it go. I was so happy that he took me on my first waterfowl hunt that I just didn't care—I was becoming a man.

● ● ● ●

16 • TALL TALES AND LOTS OF LUCK

IN 1978, I SWITCHED GEARS in my career. I was nearly 30 when I took the job at Berkley, and I'd had a good degree of success with some of my ideas; however, I wasn't that politically astute. As a result, I wasn't on the best terms with my boss, Paul. After seven years, it was clear that my salary had topped out and I could forget about putting either of my kids through college.

There was some back-and-forth negotiating, but in the end, I took a job with Hutchinson Technology Inc., in Minnesota. HTI payed me about 75% more than I had been making, plus a generous offering of shares. I also had a lot of respect for the guys I was working for. I was very impressed with their intelligence, technology, and work ethic. At that time HTI was a job-shop that manufactured computer components for anyone who needed us. At first, we would work with anything that was chemically etched, and then we moved into designing and developing suspension assemblies for disk drives. They were used in desktops, laptops, video recorders—basically any kind of digital storage device. It was pretty cutting-edge in the '80s. Eventually, HTI developed its own proprietary product line. Today, they develop suspension assemblies as well as an optical image-stabilization actuator for use in the slimmest of smartphone cameras.

I worked with HTI for over 10 years. When I started there, we had 100 employees. In just 10 years, we grew to a workforce of 3,000. It was an exciting and intense part of my career: I had so many opportunities to grow professionally.

I might have left Berkley & Co., but I still loved to fish, and with all the change and the hectic pace of life, I needed my fishing and hunting more than ever. In October of '79, I took Troy on another trip to the Chute. We also brought along my good friend Tom.

Tom was a good-looking guy who stood about six feet tall and always had a story and a laugh for you. He was an avid hunter. In fact, the first time I met him, I noticed a crescent-shaped scar over his right eye.

"I see you're a hunter," I said to him, pointing to the scar.

He lit up with the recognition and touched his scar. "You know what this is then?" he said.

"I do," I said, "I've seen that on quite a few hunters."

We were friends from there on in. As it turned out, Tom was also something of a practical joker. He'd been raised fishing and hunting, and he told Troy and me a story about when he was a boy.

"My dad brought me along ice fishing when I was a kid, around your age," he said to my 11-year-old son.

Troy leaned in, "Oh yeah?"

"We were with a bunch of his buddies and they got drinking pretty early in the day," said Tom. Then he did a great impression of his dad, "Beer keeps a guy warm!" and we laughed at the imitation. He went on, "Anyhow, so Dad and his buddies are half in-the-bag by noon and they decided it was time for me to make them sandwiches. Well, okay, so me and my cousin, Mike, cut up some bread and opened a can of sardines and made a bunch of sandwiches. I guess we did a good job because Bud, this old guy with a beard out to here," Tom gestured a beard about four feet long, "he says to me, 'Tommy-boy, that was a darn good sammich! Gimme anuther!'" Again, Troy and I laughed at his slurring, drunken imitation. He continued, "The only problem was that we used up all the sardines. We still had some bread, but no fish. Then Mike gets this look in his eye, like . . ." Tom made a face that resembled the Grinch when he got the idea to steal Christmas, " . . . and he points to the bait bucket! It's got little fish swimming around and I say, 'Nooo,' and Mike says, 'Yaaa,' then I say, 'Yaaa!' Okay, it was on!" Troy was riveted and his eyes were huge. "So, we waited a couple minutes until the old guys were looking the other way, and we both grabbed a handful of shiner minnows. You ever see a shiner minnow, Troy?" Tom asked.

"Yeah, they look just like sardines!" Troy laughed.

"Exactly like that!" said Tom. "We slapped 'em between a couple of pieces of bread and had to wait a minute for them to stop squiggling," Tom gestured holding a sandwich between two hands, shaking, like the sandwich was trying to get away. Troy giggled.

"'You bring it to him,' I say to Mike, 'No, you bring it,' he says to me. Okay, so I bring it over to ole Bud and hand it to him. 'Here you are, Bud,' I say, innocent as a babe." Tom's face looked angelic in the telling, then switched into an old grizzled character, and he said, "'Ah, good one, Tommy-boy!'" Back to his normal voice, he said, "And he takes a huge bite! Mike and I just held our breath as he chewed, waiting to see what he'd do."

"So? What'd he do?" asked Troy, hanging on every word.

"He busted out in this *huge* smile, with bread and fish in his teeth and everything, an' he says, 'Damned if this one isn't even better than the last one! Pass me a beer!'"

Troy and I both doubled over with laughter, tears streaming down our eyes. Even Tom was belly-laughing over his own story.

So that's the kind of guy Tom was: a good guy to be around.

On this trip, we were out hunting around Ogani Lake and we came across a few other guys' camp. We stopped by to say hello and while we were having a cup of coffee, Tom noticed that they had an abundance of walleyes in the tub.

"Now that's what you call a mess-a-fish," said Tom. "Where'd you find that many 'eyes?"

One of the hunters replied, "Just south of that small island on the east end of the lake."

"Is that right? You mind telling me what you used?" asked Tom.

The hunter dropped Tom's eye and glanced at a couple of the other guys, who looked suddenly uncomfortable. Then the hunter said, "Well . . . I guess we used a square hook."

Tom was confused but decided not to press the point. He just nodded. It was obvious that something about the question made the men uncomfortable. We passed the rest of the short visit companionably and then carried on with our moose hunting.

It wasn't long before we shot a bull and had it hanging on the meat rack, cooling. It was snowing by then, so it wouldn't take long to cool, but Tom suggested that while we waited, we take a trip out to where the other hunters had caught so many walleyes.

"I could eat a walleye dinner tonight," he said.

"Yeah, so could I," I said. So, the three of us got into the canoe and headed out.

We motored up behind the island and stopped the engine. While Tom was readying his line with a bucktail jig, he asked me, "Gary, do you know what that guy meant by a 'square hook'?"

I nodded and had to smile, "He meant they used a gill net."

"Aw!" Tom spat with disgust, "That's just cheatin'!" With that, he cast his line and caught a walleye right away. In fact, we all caught our limits in about half-an-hour. Who needed square hooks?

With a bucketful of fish, we headed back to camp. Cold and damp, we wanted a fire to warm up by.

"Hey Troy," said Tom, with mischief in his eye. "I'll bet you can't split that log with one chop."

"That little thing?" said Troy, never one to back away from a challenge. "Easy!"

"Little? That's not little. And look here, there's a big knot in the middle of it. No way. It'll take you at least three hits," said Tom.

"Nope," said Troy, his young manhood affronted. "I can do it in one."

"Oh yeah? Want to put your money where your mouth is?" said Tom.

"Yeah, I do! I'll bet you a buck I can split that in one hit," said Troy.

"A buck! You got a buck?" asked Tom.

"Yeah. Do you?" Troy asked, as though Tom might not be good for it.

Tom reached into his pocket and pulled out a damp dollar bill and handed it to me, "You hold our money, Gary."

Troy, seeing that, ran into his tent and came out with a dollar, which he handed to me. I accepted it and gravely folded it with the other and put them in my shirt pocket.

"I just sharpened that axe, Troy. That should give you an advantage," I said.

"That's good," said Troy seriously as he hefted the tool up and down a couple of times to judge the weight. Then he placed the blade in the middle of the log, looked at Tom and said, "Ready?"

"Anytime you are," Tom said.

Troy raised the ax above his head and then brought it down with a mighty blow.

I have no doubt that he could have split that log right in two with one strike, had he actually hit the log. Instead, he cleaved his own boot! The ax penetrated the upper leather and the rubber sole right between his big toe and second toe. It was sheer luck that he didn't put the ax right through his foot. The only damage was to his boot—and, of course, to his pride.

● ● ● ●

17 ● WOODCHUCKER

TROY'S MISHAP WITH CHOPPING WOOD reminds me of one of my own firewood mishap when I was a kid.

One day, I was helping my dad unload firewood from a hay rack. I was standing on the rack throwing the wood onto a pile; my dad would then pick it up and stack it neatly. I remember picking up a split chunk of wood and tossing it toward the pile. Somehow in mid-air the wood took a detour and hit my dad right in the head! I could not believe I did that! Dad spun away and doubled over, holding his head. When I saw a stream of blood pouring from between his fingers, my own blood ran cold.

"Dad! I'm sorry!" I cried. He didn't even look at me but strode off to the house for first aid. I figured I was in some serious trouble. I felt terrible, and I was not sure of what the consequences of this unfortunate event might be. I did, however, know that I wanted to get the heck out of Dodge. So, I grabbed a shovel and a found an out-of-the-way spot in the yard with sandy soil and started digging. In almost no time at all I had managed to dig a hole deep enough to hide in. No one had declared war on me, but I wasn't taking any chances. I hunkered down in fear and misery for the rest of the day. Looking back on it, I wish that I'd heard General Patton's admonition: If you're digging a foxhole, you're digging your own grave.

Eventually, I heard Ma calling me, "GAARY! Come and get your supper!"

Is this a trick? Are they trying to lure me in? Is this some kind of battle strategy? Starve the enemy all day long and then smoke him out with the smell of roast beef and apple pie? If it is a trick, it's a darned good one! Carefully, I made my way to the house. With each step, I did battle internally. With my left foot forward I was thinking, *Mmmm . . . dinner.* With my right foot forward I was thinking, *I'm in sooo much trouble.* Left: dinner. Right: trouble. Left. Right. Dinner. Trouble. It was a very long walk to the table.

I took off my dirty boots, washed my dirty hands, and as nonchalantly as possible I slid into my seat at the table. Carefully, ever so carefully, I raised my eyes to peek at my dad who hadn't yet sat down. He was fussing with something on the counter. There was a bandage on his forehead, but his eyes were sparkling with good spirits. When we'd all gathered at the table and were sitting, Ma said grace, and no one said anything about the wood chucking incident. The whole foxhole experience made for a long and difficult day, but it never turned out to be a "grave" mistake because it taught me a good lesson: instead of hiding from adversity in a hole of your own making, it's better to face it straight up.

● ● ● ●

18 • A GOOD DEAL?

MY BUDDY QUINT HAD A ritual where he met up with some guys every morning for coffee at a local restaurant in Rochester, Minnesota, called, Gramma's Kitchen. One morning, he got talking with his friend, Fenske, about hunting up in the Wenasaga Lake area.

"We've bagged a moose just about every time we're there," Quint told Fenske.

"Is that right?" said Fenske. "I've got a favorite hunting place too. It's up by Rice Lake, Ontario."

"Really? Have you got anything really big?" asked Quint.

"Oh yeah. Last year I got a beautiful bull, and the year before that I got a good-sized cow," said Fenske.

"Maybe I should give it try," said Quint.

"Definitely. As a matter of fact, I have a friend with a resort on Rice Lake who could guide for you," said Fenske.

"Oh yeah?" said Quint. "Where did you say it is?"

"Rice Lake, Ontario. It's in the southwest corner of the province, near the Manitoba border. Just north of Lake of the Woods. It's a little remote but in a perfect location as far as I'm concerned. It's quiet there, and the fishing and hunting are excellent. Ralph has owned it for a while, but he's got some health issues and is looking at selling," said Fenske.

"Sounds like you found a good spot," said Quint. Just then,

the waitress came with their breakfast and the conversation moved to other topics.

Later that day, Quint picked up the phone and called me. "Gary, how do you feel about taking the family to Rice Lake, Ontario for some fishing and hunting?"

Quint still lived in Rochester, Minnesota, while I had moved to Spirit Lake, Iowa, but the distance never mattered much. We kept in touch by phone and did many trips together every year. "Rice Lake? Tell me about it," I said. It sounded like it might be a good sidetrack to take.

"I was talking to my buddy, Fenske, and he was telling me about a resort there that's for sale. He said it's good hunting grounds, and the lake is full of walleyes. I guess the guy only wants $10,000 for it," said Quint.

"Are you thinking about buying it?" I asked. It wouldn't have surprised me. Quint was an insurance agent by day, but his true love in life was fishing and hunting. I could see him running a lodge. I had half a mind to go in on it with him.

"I'm thinking about it, but even if I decided not to buy, it'll be a great holiday for us," he said.

"Sounds good, I'll talk to Ginny."

Ginny was excited about the prospect of taking the kids on a trip. I let Quint know we were good-to-go.

"Okay, I'll give Fenske a call and get Ralph's number." So, Quint called Fenske, but it was Fenske's wife who picked up the phone.

"Hello, Anne, it's Quint. Is Fenske there?" asked Quint.

"No, I'm afraid he isn't. Is there anything I can help with?" she asked.

"Maybe. Fenske was telling me about a guy with a resort up in Rice Lake, Ontario. I think he said the name was Ralph. I wonder if you can get me his number?" Quint asked.

"Oh sure, Ralph Bilton. Hang on, I'll go get it," said Anne.

After a moment, she came back on the line, "Here it is . . ." and she gave him the number. Then, Quint called Ralph and arranged for a party of eight—four adults and four children—to stay at the resort and do some fishing and hunting. Also, he let him know that he would be interested in seeing the resort as a prospective buyer.

We each loaded our families, gear, and canoes and embarked on the 11-hour drive. Interstates gave way to highways, which became mere roads by the time we reached the small town of Redditt, Ontario. Ralph met us at the small train station there, where we transferred our gear and canoes to the mail car. This was the main east-west passenger train in Canada. It was kind of fun to take the train, even if it was only a 30-minute trip north. We unloaded at the Rice Lake stop. We were extremely remote by this time: The Rice Lake "depot" was a shack with a phone to call the train for pickup. If you didn't call ahead, it'd go right by. The forest was dense, and the roads were more like game trails.

From the Rice Lake stop, we portaged our canoes about a quarter of a mile to the lake. The mosquitos were thick and we were all slapping away at them.

"Mom, I think I need more bug lotion, do you have it?" my daughter Dawn asked Ginny.

As she rummaged in her pack for the bottle, I said, "The only reasonable mosquito repellant here is a shotgun."

This made Dawn laugh. Then Troy piped up, "The mosquitos here are so tough that when you slap 'em, they slap you back!"

That made all of us laugh. Dawn came up with, "You can't just swat them, you have to get the SWAT team on 'em."

I said, "The Ontario government had to account for the density of the flock when issuing the Air Quality Index numbers." That got a groan.

Ginny said, "Didn't I see a sign back there on the highway that said 'Caution, Mosquitoes Crossing'?"

And on it went, the Oberg Family Vacation. None of us could have predicted how vicous the little beasts would be (the mosquitoes, not my family), but although the kids made it crystal clear that they were being "eaten alive," they didn't complain too much. I gave them both WWII military hats with bug nets, so they didn't fare too badly. Ginny, like most everything she does, took it all in stride.

My uncle Sven was a Swede who immigrated to the US when he was 20. He was the consummate fisherman. I don't know if he brought his fishing skill with him at that age, or if he learned it in the lakes and rivers here, but he was good. He also came up with a clever idea for protecting himself from mosquitos and deer flies. He would tuck his pant legs into his socks and then slide his feet into plastic grocery bags and duct tape them closed around his shins. Uncle Sven was a resourceful guy. I would have used his technique with the aggressive Rice Lake mosquitoes, but I didn't have seven plastic grocery bags to go around.

We paddled another half mile across the lake to get to the resort. The resort consisted of a log lodge and three log cabins. The kids had a great time, despite the mosquitoes, and we all did a lot of fishing and exploring.

Quint and I had a good look at the place through the eyes of an owner. There were pros and cons. I loved the rustic nature, but it was terribly remote. I liked that it was excellent hunting grounds and that the lake was so full of fish, but there weren't many cabins, and they weren't in great shape. Plus, the winters there were long, long, long. Realistically, how many days per year could we keep them rented?

Aside from the business ponderings, it was a great holiday, that's for certain.

On the day before we left, Ralph asked us if we wanted to take any fish home with us. Of course, I said yes. The next morning, I woke up to find a tub chockablock full of walleyes. I couldn't believe how many fish were in there! Ralph must have been fishing for hours and hours to catch that many. Did he have a magic lure?

"Ralph! How in the world did you catch this many 'eyes?" I asked.

He winked and said, "Square hook."

I had to laugh. No wonder I couldn't imagine a magic fishing lure; there wasn't such a thing. A gill net felt like cheating; however, I had to admit it was very effective.

As much fun as we'd had at Rice Lake, Quint was not interested in buying the resort. We returned home with a lot of fish and a lot of good memories. I figured it was still a good deal.

Quint later told me about a conversation he had with his buddy, Fenske, the next time they met at Gramma's Kitchen.

"Fenske!" shouted Quint the moment he saw him, sticking out his hand.

Fenske looked a little bewildered at such an enthusiastic greeting on such an average morning, but took Quint's outstretched hand and shook it anyway, "Quint?" he asked.

"I can't thank you enough. We just got back from Rice Lake. I took the whole family, and a buddy of mine brought his too. We had a great time!"

The two sat at their usual table with some of the other guys, Fenske's face broke into a wide smile, "Is that so?"

"Oh yes," said Quint, "After you told me about how great it was there, I had to see for myself. I was thinking that I might just buy the place. We had a great time, but after talking it over with my wife, we decided that we should stay here, at least until the kids are out of school."

Fenske's jaw dropped open and his eyes grew wider and wider as Quint talked. "You—you were going to—to buy the resort?" he stammered.

"Yeah, I gave it some thought. I may have too. It's a great price, but it's just not the right time for us," said Quint.

"Did you know that I've been thinking about buying it, too?" asked Fenske.

"You what?" said Quint, alarmed.

"Yeah, I've had my eye on it now for months," said Fenske.

"Oh wow. I had no idea! I never meant to go behind your back," said Quint, who was very concerned now; his mouth agape and eyes huge. Quint was a man of integrity and the idea that he had almost scooped a business opportunity at the expense of a friend was horrifying to him.

"I mean—how did you even get Ralph's phone number?" asked Fenske.

"I called to get it from you, but you were out, so Anne gave it to me," said Quint.

"That woman! I'm gonna kill her!" said Fenske.

A week later, Fenske bought the Rice Lake resort. He spent several years guiding and fishing in the area. It sounds like a happy ending for Fenske, but unfortunately, it was not. One night, Fenske left camp and never came back. The authorities searched for days, but he was never heard from again. I sometimes wonder if that might have been Quint's fate if he had bought the resort. Probably not, but it does get me thinking about the big questions.

● ● ● ●

19 • LOW CHARACTERS

WHEN I LOOK BACK AT some of my most favorite fishing and hunting places over the years, I always think of the Chute, the Boundary Waters Canoe Area, and Lake of the Woods (LOW). If you added up all the days I've spent at Lake of the Woods, you'd come up with about a year of my life.

Lake of the Woods is a very big lake, with 14,552 islands and about 65,000 miles of shoreline. It's the largest lake in the USA, after the five Great Lakes, although it's not entirely located in the USA. It's positioned at the junction of Minnesota (south), Manitoba (northwest), and Ontario (northeast). The USA, Canada, Manitoba, and Ontario governments all cooperate in its management.

People have widely believed, and even published, that the lake level rose 12 feet with the building of a couple dams in the northern part, but the truth is that the lake has always had rather extreme ups and downs. Yes, the dams did raise the water levels, but only by about three feet. Since they built the dams, the water levels have naturally fluctuated by as much as seven feet, depending on weather. Since I started going to the lake in the 1980s, I've seen the levels go up and down, although never by seven feet.

While the dams may have affected locals, I can't say they've had any effect on the fun we've always had on our trips. In fact, I'd say tourism is alive and well. For several years, I'd take family and friends there for some serious, quality vacationing. We would drive to the US-Canada border, and continue north for another two hours until arriving at the small town of Sioux Narrows, Ontario. There, I'd go and find Jim, the owner of Floating Lodges houseboat rental company. He'd set us up with a houseboat—but not just an ordinary houseboat—a floating lodge. Our usual rental was a 60-foot long, double decker, floating lodge. The boat had 12 double beds in six separate sleeping areas, two sofa beds, 2½ bathrooms, 2½ fridges, a chest freezer, a 120V generator, a full-size kitchen, dishwasher, microwave, two barbecues, a water slide, and was powered by twin 120HP Volvo engines. This was vacationing in style!

Generally, we'd have 10-15 people along, and with that many bodies you get a lot of characters. Once everyone was aboard, we'd leave the dock and head west about 15-25 miles before finding some nice beach and launching our small boats. Predominantly we were going for walleye, but sometimes we'd catch small-mouth bass or northern pike. Some years, when we got there within two weeks of ice-out, we could catch lake trout. They tend to like about 52-degrees. Any warmer than that and they go deep, making them hard to find.

Everyone has a great time at Lake of the Woods. Everyone has their own personality, their own likes, strengths, weaknesses, sense of humor. For instance, there was Durwood who came along for several years. He was probably the smallest guy aboard, but he had the biggest heart, and was hands-down the best fisherman in the bunch. Even with those kinds of bragging rights, he never took himself too seriously. Once, we were on the beach on the east end of Yellow Girl Bay; there were about eight of us all standing around the fire. The sun had dropped below the horizon, but it was still early dusk. It had been a successful day of fishing, and we had a big dump of fish guts on a pile of rocks nearby. Someone happened to look up to see a bald eagle circling us, clearly eying the fish guts. Durwood piped up and said, "Uh-oh! I'm the smallest guy here. I'm getting the hell out!" and he made a beeline for the houseboat. We all doubled with laughter!

One year, we had a couple of real characters aboard: Jack and Earl. These guys had been friends their whole life and had learned a neat prank back when they were kids in Boy Scouts, which they decided to play on Frank, a friend from Germany. I guess Jack and Earl figured he would make an excellent target since he was good-humored, was unfamiliar with the local wildlife, and would have no knowledge of old Boy Scout tricks.

As a rite of passage, a new kid in the Scouts would be told that everyone was going on a snipe hunt. Now, the snipe is a notoriously difficult bird to catch. It's a nervous little thing with an erratic flight pattern, which makes it extremely hard to shoot. In fact, that's where the term "sniper" came from—it refers to a sharpshooter who typically shoots from a camouflaged location. So, instead of shooting it, the new kid is told to quietly approach the snipe when it's on the ground, with a stick as well as a bag. He should hold the bag open, low on the ground. He should then make a "peep, peep" noise to coax the snipe into the bag. If the snipe doesn't walk right into the bag, he should at least whack it with the stick. Then, while the new kid crouches there with the bag and stick, the other kids sneak away—which is where the term "stuck holding the bag" comes from. Really, it's a time-honored tradition.

Frank, being the trusting, unsuspecting target, believed Jack when he pointed and said, "I know of a nearly foolproof way of catching those snipes over there."

"Oh!" said Frank, "Is zat right?"

"Sure. Hey, Earl! Do you remember how we used to catch

snipe back when we were in the Boy Scouts?" Jack said with a sidelong wink.

Earl, catching on immediately, said, "Oh yeah. With a bag and stick."

"That's right," said Jack, "with a bag and stick."

Frank wasn't sure what to make of that. He'd never heard of catching a bird that way before, "How does zat work?" he asked. After Jack and Earl explained the process to him, he said, "No . . . really? Are you maykink a joke for me?"

It was as if Jack and Earl lost 30 years and they were suddenly the fresh, not-so-innocent Boy Scouts they once were, "Not at all, Frank. It's true! That's the best way to catch a snipe."

Frank looked to the rest of us guys for confirmation that he wasn't getting bamboozled, but we all went along with the ruse and nodded. "Oh yes," we said. So, Frank decided that this must be true. We all searched the floating lodge for a right bag and stick and watched, smirking, as Jack and Earl led Frank ashore for a snipe hunt.

It wasn't long before Jack and Earl returned without Frank.

"Where's Frank?" someone asked.

Earl said, "We left him holding the bag!" and he burst out laughing.

Jack doubled over, crying with laughter. "He's all—hah—all crouched down in the woods—haa haa haa— with that bag, going 'Peep, peep' at every bird that comes near him! Haaaa!"

That cracked us all up. We laughed long and hard at our own cleverness. I wondered how Frank would take it when he discovered we'd all tricked him. He seemed like a laid-back guy with a good sense of humor. I hoped he would see it as just a lot of fun between friends.

About a half-hour later, Frank showed up. He'd removed his muddy boots outside and stood in his socks in the doorway where we were all sitting around, grinning, waiting to see what he was going to do. He had a huge smile on his face! I felt relieved that he didn't get angry about the joke.

He walked in his stockinged feet over to Jack and Earl. They weren't sure what was coming. They expected anger, indignation, outraged offence, or at least a little annoyance—they didn't expect a smile so big it looked like it might just jump off his face and sing us a song. Frank said, "Sank you! Vat a vonderful technique. Ze guys back at Germany are going to not believe zis!" Then he opened the bag to reveal one dead grouse.

Jack and Earl's jaws dropped.

The rest of us burst out into peals of laughter! The joke was on the tricksters! Well done Frank, well done! We all slapped Frank on the back and congratulated him. Jack and Earl, although they couldn't believe it, congratulated him on his hunting prowess and praised his skills. Their trick had backfired on them, but there would still be game on the table that night.

Oddly enough, it turned out Frank must have had some mad voodoo-magic skills, because the following year—still not knowing that he'd been "tricked"—he used the same technique and caught yet another grouse. We never expected it to work on a snipe, but we sure never expected it to work on a grouse, either. Maybe he's like the Pied Piper, or the Horse Whisperer, only for grouse.

Not everyone aboard was as easy-going as Frank, however. There were a couple of older guys who reminded me a lot of John and Max from that movie *Grumpy Old Men* played by Jack Lemmon and Walter Matthau. Our "Max" was an old guy named Bill. He was the Cargill grain elevator manager and had to deal with a constant barrage of disgruntled farmers. It must have worn off on him over the years because he himself was very disgruntled.

Bill would be sitting at the front of the boat with his head down and chin forward and someone would ask him, "How're you doin' Bill?"

To which he would reply, "Well, my high-school daughter's pregnant, my wife has a cancerous brain tumor, my son just outed himself to me, my other son lives in the basement in a boar's nest, and corn's under two bucks a bushel!" Then he'd look at the asker and add sarcastically, "Other than that, things are just great, thanks for asking."

Guy was to Bill as John was to Max. They were good friends, but you'd never know it. What a pair! One year they got so deep into the argument that Bill flat-out refused to drive up to Lake of the Woods with Guy. I thought we'd have to do an intervention to clear things up, but once they both got to the lake, the fresh Canadian air, the ample elbow room, and the big fish mellowed the two of them out enough that they tolerated each other again. A walleye war was avoided. It's hard to stay miserable at Lake of the Woods.

● ● ● ●

The houseboat we rent when we go to the Lake of the Woods.

20 • ODE TO DUCT TAPE

DUCT TAPE IS NOT ONLY an essential tool for plumbers, tailors, pilots, mechanics, and romantics everywhere—it's essential for fishermen and hunters too. The silver bond is more critical than bullets and possibly more critical than toilet paper. It's a must-pack item for every outdoorsman. I am constantly amazed at its versatility and usefulness. I was on a trip with a friend once who had to tape half his snowmobile together. He's often said, "We're not havin' fun if we're not wrecking s**t!" Now, we call him Duct Tape Dale. I have another friend who gave his girl a bouquet of wildflowers with the stems all duct taped together. He declared to her, "If you can't find me handsome, at least you can find me handy!" If only I held the patent.

In previous years, when hunting in the Wenasaga Lake area, we sometimes brought along a 14-foot aluminum Crestliner boat and a 25-horsepower Evenrude engine in addition to two or three smaller canoes, each with their own smaller engines. It was great to have the bigger boat and engine because it allowed us to cover more ground during the peak moose-spotting times. However, hauling the aluminum and big outboard made the trip onerous instead of just challenging, especially if we were carrying a lot of meat back out. To take some of the weight, we sometimes hired a plane to carry some of our cargo between Wenasaga Lake and the Chute. In 1980, Quint, Tom, me, and my friend Jim, decided we'd portage the aluminum and outboard, two canoes, and all our gear both ways, but we would hire a plane to haul out any meat.

We made our way up the Wenasaga River, portaging around waterfalls and rapids. At that age, I was strong enough to carry the engine on my own. I tucked a pad between the engine and my shoulder and hauled it all the way. Twice, the cowling of the engine fell off, exposing the guts. I had to set the engine down and put the wayward lid back on. We probably should have just duct taped the thing down. Why not? I was using duct tape to keep a tackle box closed. I'd used it to create a makeshift strap for a bag, and I had it wrapped around my lower pant legs to keep the mosquitos from feeding on my legs, per my old uncle Sven's recipe.

Finally, we made it to the Chute and set up camp.

Jim was gung-ho about getting out hunting, so once we had everything stowed, he said, "Why don't Tom and I take the boat and check out Whitemud Lake?"

Tom replied, "Great idea! The shores of Whitemud look very 'moosey' today."

They threw a bunch of gear into the boat and headed for the lake. Jim steered from the back of the boat, sitting just to the left of the engine, while Tom sat further forward and just to the right, to keep the boat balanced. Generally, everyone took turns sitting in front, since it's the best shooting position.

The sky was deep blue, the wind was calm, and the water was glassy. Jim and Tom couldn't carry a conversation over the drone of the engine during the long ride to the lake, but even in silence, it's hard to carry a conversation over the beauty of the place.

As soon as the narrow waterways opened to the vastness of the lake, Jim shouted, "Let's open 'er up! I want to cover some ground!"

Tom nodded to Jim and made a show of holding on. Jim

opened the throttle, causing the engine to dig into the water, and the bow of the boat to point high. After a moment the boat leveled off and they were skimming along the lake's surface. It was exhilarating: wind in the hair, the boat flying along the water. It was one of those perfect moments, the kind that makes your chest expand right along with your spirit. Tom pointed toward a tall tree with three eagles perched high, and Jim steered a little closer to see them. And that's when it happened.

Tom was joyfully soaking in the magnificence of the birds, the beauty of the day, and the thrill of the ride when suddenly he was brained from behind and thrown forward into the bow of the little boat. At first, he thought Jim must have hit him in the head, but why would he go and do that?

"Jim! What the—?" he said. Fortunately, his head happened to be as hard as brass, so the braining merely rang his bell. He shook it off and rearranged his limbs back into a sitting position. Once he got himself up, he realized that it couldn't have been Jim who cracked him in the skull. The boat had come to a standstill, and Jim was sprawled out mid-ship, trying to disentangle himself from several bags of gear. He was looking up at Tom with a bewildered expression.

"What happened?" asked Jim.

"What are you asking me for? You were driving!" said Tom. He reached a hand out to help Jim into a sitting position on the bench that ran across the middle of the boat. Jim took it gratefully and sat, wincing, gently touching his right rib cage. "Are you okay?" asked Tom.

"Yeah, I'm okay," said Jim with a grimace. "I might have bruised a couple ribs, though."

"What hit me?" asked Tom, rubbing the back of his head.

Jim reached across him and picked up the motor's cowling. "This."

"Uh . . . ?" said Tom, "How did the cowling hit me in the head?" It was a really big cowling and not exactly light.

"We must have hit a rock that was deep enough for the boat to pass over, but not the skeg of the engine. We were motoring along when the engine kicked, and the cowling flew off and hit your head. I got thrown forward." Jim added, "Are you okay?"

Tom felt the quickly rising lump on the back of his noggin and said wryly, "Ya. It was just my head. I don't use it much anyway."

Jim smiled and said, "Pass me the lid." Tom handed the cowling over and Jim placed it atop the exposed engine, noting the broken latch that would have secured it there. "I wonder if this thing'll start?"

He checked that the engine could still move from side-to-side, adjusted the throttle to half-way, and gave a pull on the starter cord.

Blrrrm— It turned over but never caught. Jim, however, lit up with pain. Groaning, he sat down on the bench, holding his ribs.

"Here, let me try," said Tom. He moved to the back of the boat and got a good grip on the cord then gave a mighty pull.

Blrrrm—

Muttering under his breath, Tom gave another three pulls in quick succession.

Blrrrm— *Blrrrm*— *Blrrrm*—

Breathing hard with the effort, Tom said, "Not good," and sat down. The two men looked at each other and then at the vast wilderness around them. What had been a pleasant journey by boat would be a long paddle back.

One of the eagles issued its sweet, high call.

"Maybe it's just overheated," said Jim. "Let's give it a minute and try again."

Tom nodded and rubbed the back of his head. It was starting

to throb all over. They were drifting along the shore. At that lazy pace, it was easy to see the rocks lurking just below the surface. It was disturbing; like walking through a lovely meadow on a blue-sky day, only to realize you're strolling through an overgrown cemetery. Tom shivered and said, "I'm going to try it again."

Blrrrm— Blrrrm— Blrrrm—

"Is the key on?" asked Jim.

"Yup," said Tom.

"Is there fuel in the line?"

Tom squeezed the fuel ball and found it hard, "Yup."

"Are we losing any fuel out the back?" asked Jim.

Tom looked over the back of the boat for the telltale rainbow-sheen of fuel on water, "Nope."

"Is the choke in?"

"Aha!" said Tom, "The choke is out. It must have been knocked when we hit." He pushed the knob back into the engine. It popped right back out. "Well . . ." He pushed it in, it popped back out. "Pass me the duct tape."

Jim rummaged around in a bag for a time. "Hah!" he cried as he pulled the silver ring from the bag and passed it to Tom.

Tom taped the choke in the *off* position and stood up to face the engine again. Rubbing the lump on his head, he decided to duct tape the cowling down, too. Then, he took hold of the starter rope, sent up a little prayer, and pulled for all he was worth.

VrrrOOOOMM!

Both guys let out a WHOOP of joy and relief.

Tom said, "Okay! Let's just hope that it keeps running all the way back. I'll steer. Can you get up to the bow and guide us around the rocks until we're clear?"

"Will do." Jim moved forward, guiding them away from the watery cemetery.

Tom headed back to the river much more slowly than they came. Once they made the right-hand turn back into the Wenasaga River, they had to work their way back upstream to the Chute. Every time the engine made any change in sound, they'd hold their breath for a moment. The closer they got to the Chute, the more tension drained from them, but it was still a worrisome ride back.

They finally beached the boat, and Quint and I went down to greet them. "How'd it go?" I asked, hoping to hear they'd at least found fresh sign of moose.

"Well," Jim and Tom looked at each other and then told us the story. I moved to have a look at the engine.

"Wow," said Quint, "I'm glad you made it back safe. You got lucky today!"

"Don't we know it?" said Jim.

"Actually, I think you got luckier than you realize," I called from my place behind the boat. "Check it out."

The other three came to look at the engine where I was pointing. "See the crack?" There was a crack in the front of the motor's skeg, leaking a little bit of oil.

"There's not much oil leaking now because there's not much left to leak. It's practically drained," I said.

Tom said, "If that crack was just a little bigger and lost oil any faster . . ."

Jim added, "Or if we had gone much further along the lake . . ."

I finished the thought, "The lower unit would have completely seized, and you'd have been paddling back."

Later that evening, around the fire, we talked about what to do with the engine.

"I say we bring it back to Ear Falls and get someone to repair it," said Jim.

Tom nodded, "It's only our first day out. We have a week to go. It would be a shame if we had to do it without the boat."

I understood where he was coming from. That year, the Ministry had moved the season back a week, to avoid the rut, so the moose were not responding to calls. We'd need every advantage we could get if we wanted a successful hunt.

"Someone would lose a day of hunting," said Jim.

"Yeah, but we're so much more restricted without it. Our chances of bagging a moose are way lower," said Quint. "I want to hunt, but I also want to kill a moose."

Then Tom said, "I wonder if we could just patch it with duct tape?"

I thought about that. "You know, we probably could."

"Yeah, we could clean the oil off the paint and put a few wraps around the leg. I'll bet that would hold just fine until we get it back to Minnesota," said Quint.

"And it very well could," I said, "but we run a greater risk of losing oil, and I didn't bring much extra."

We all fell silent for a few moments and watched the fire spit sparks into the night sky.

"You know, Quint," I said. "I have a friend who hit a rock with his brand new 60-horsepower Johnson on his first day out. He was fishing on the Lake of the Woods and was in way too deep to get it out easily. He did just what you said—he wrapped it up with duct tape and carried on like nothing ever happened. He ran it for a week."

Quint nodded and said, "Didn't you tell me about a time you fixed the actual boat with duct tape?"

I remembered the incident and smiled, "Yeah. A friend's StarCraft aluminum boat on Leech Lake. It developed a three-foot stress crack just under the splash rail. We did the same thing you just suggested. We cleaned and dried the area, then ran about three layers of duct tape on both sides of the hull. Fished for a week after that with no problems."

Jim, who was likely still shaken from the day's near-miss, said, "Yeah, but I think it's a bit risky to rely on just duct tape when a welder is available in Ear Falls. Two guys would lose a day's hunting, but the other two can keep at it here."

We pondered that as sparks from the fire disguised themselves as stars.

"What do you think, Gary?" asked Jim.

"Well," I said, "I think you're right. I prefer calculated risks, and this isn't a risk we need to take. Two of us should take it back to Ear Falls in the morning and see what can be done."

"I'll go," said Quint.

"Okay, that's decided. Quint and I will take it back to Ear Falls tomorrow and see if we can find a welder," I said. "Jim and Tom, you stay here to hold down the fort and see if you can shoot a local moose."

The next morning, well before the sun came up, Quint and I put the damaged 25-horsepower into a canoe outfitted with one of the smaller motors, and made our way downstream. We portaged around all the necessary spots and tied up to the landing, but we still had to haul the heavy engine about 10 miles to get to the nearest mechanic with welding capabilities. It was just after noon by the time we got there.

The mechanic was about five-foot, eight-inches, and must have weighed about 350 pounds. He had a large, round nose with the telltale blue veins of a hard drinker, and long, thinning hair. "Howdy," he said. He pulled a rag out of his back pocket, wiped his hand, and thrust it toward us. "Bill."

We shook, then explained the problem. As Bill listened to us talk, he slowly walked around the engine like a sculptor might walk around a raw mass of marble that was waiting to be fashioned into a masterpiece. He leaned over and peered at the crack. He rubbed his finger into it, and then rubbed the oil between his thumb and forefinger. Then suddenly, he stood up and said, "Nope."

I blinked. "What do you mean?"

"I mean, it can't be welded," said Bill.

"Sure it can," said Quint, "it's metal isn't it?"

Bill looked sidelong at Quint and said, "Yyyes, it's metal, but welding would just make a mess of it. I don't think it would hold, and it would look terrible." Then he added, "You can just wrap it with some duct tape for now and look for replacement parts when you get home." Quint and I laughed. Bill looked confused.

"I say something funny?" he asked.

"I'm not too worried about how it's going to look," I said. "All I want is for the crack to be sealed. You can try welding the edges together, or you can weld a patch over it, whatever. Just plug the hole," I said.

I once watched a guy weld two aluminum pop cans together, so I was pretty sure that Bill, despite his artistic sensibilities, could manage to close a crack in this aluminum engine.

Bill looked skeptical and started his circling again. Almost to himself, he muttered, "Maybe . . ."

"I just want to get it fixed so I can get back to my moose," said Quint. "My moose is waiting for me somewhere on the shore of Ogani Lake, and I need a boat to get to him."

This made Bill chuckle and he said, "Well, I guess I could give it a try."

"There's the fighting spirit!" said Quint, clapping Bill on the back.

"Leave it with me," said Bill. "There's a coffee shop a few blocks that way," he gestured with his chin. "Ask for the Mega-burger, it's good."

We did as ordered. Bill was right, the meal was excellent. We gave him an hour and then paid for our food. When we got back to the shop, we found that Bill had done a fine, albeit not artistic, job of welding the break. We thanked him, paid him, and motored the boat back to camp. It was dark when we finally got there, but not that late.

The next morning, it was Quint's and my turn to take the boat to Whitemud. The sky was dark, and the morning stars were still twinkling when I got into the stern and gave Quint the bow. There was a thin line of light just skimming the treed horizon. I thought I might have detected the faint smell of impending winter, but it was still some distance away. The day had promise.

But promises get broken.

Just downstream from camp there was a tricky bend in the river. It was clearly shallow in several places, and the water rushed over boulders near the surface. It wasn't somewhere we would typically portage, but it was a place to slow down and use caution, which is exactly what I did. So, I was going quite slowly when I nailed that big rock.

"Oh—COME on!" I said, exasperated, as the boat bobbed its way through the rest of the bend—sans horsepower. I tilted the engine so the leg and prop were out of harm's way. Quint grabbed the oars and guided us to calmer water. It wasn't long before we cleared the tricky spot and were able to inspect for damage.

"Well?" asked Quint as I ran my hand down the front aspect of the leg, feeling for breaks. Aside from the ugly weld of yesterday, and some chipped paint, it seemed okay.

"Looks okay to me," I reported.

"How about the prop?" asked Quint.

I inspected the propeller for chips, dings, or bends, but I saw no damage.

"I think we dodged a bullet," I said, with no small amount of relief. I felt elated all over again. This was still going to be a good day. The river widened, and I said to Quint, "Hold on!" and cracked open the throttle. It was very responsive and in seconds, I had it up on step, skimming along the glassy green water. I was so relieved that the engine hadn't been damaged. It felt so good—the wind in the hair, the fresh air.

Then came the grind-crunch-grind-groan-sput-sput-sputter and sudden death of the engine. We had only made it about 300 yards from camp.

"Bullet—direct hit," said Quint, pessimistically, realistically.

"Hm—" I tipped the engine up and inspected the lower unit. I could tell the gear unit was frozen solid. Shot. I groaned my displeasure.

"Well?" asked Quint.

"The gears are toast," I said. "We're rowing back."

Quint put his back into the task of rowing upstream the 300 yards back to camp. We beached it, and there it sat for the rest of the hunting trip. In fact, it would be the last time we ever brought the Crestliner or that engine to the Wenasaga. It was a good thing we still had two canoes with us. It meant limiting our range, but as it turned out, there were enough local moose to satisfy everyone.

In fact, we limited out before the plane was due to arrive, so we mostly hung around camp the last couple days. It was around noon on the second-to-last day, when three Canadians passed right by our camp, portaging over the Chute on their way to Ogani Lake.

"Afternoon," one said.

"Hi there!" I replied.

We made our introductions all around, "I'm Gary, this is Quint, Jim, and that's Tom."

"I'm Dave, this is Trevor, and that's Rob," said Dave.

"Would you like a coffee? We've got some black tea if you prefer," I said.

"Yeah, thanks! I'll take a coffee," said Dave.

The three men left their aluminum boat tied to a tree with the gear sitting nearby on the beach—they were halfway through their portage.

Trevor, sitting on a log, noticed our meat pole; it was hard to miss. "Wow, that's quite the pile there. You get all that just around here or did you have to go further away?"

Quint said, "We got them all within canoeing range. We brought the 25-horse," he nodded at the dead outboard on the back of my Crestliner, "but we killed that before we killed any moose. It forced us to stay a bit closer to home."

"Well," said Trevor, "we haven't seen a single moose in the three days we've been out here." Dave and Rob nodded confirmation. "It's like they know we're comin' or something."

"Yeah!" said Rob, "Where are they?"

Tom, who was sitting quietly nearby, listening to all this, nonchalantly said, "There's one now." He nodded across the bay to where a moose was strolling out of the woods, not 400 yards away.

"Wha—?" All three Canucks turned in the direction Tom nodded. They watched, open-mouthed, as the bull moose casually decided that would be a good place to lie down. He bent his front legs and went down on his knees, then his hind end soon followed and he settled in, just as pleased as could be. Once he was hunkered in like that, we could barely make out his antlers above the tall, brown grass.

Then, all three Canadians dropped their cups, jumped to their feet, and started running for the boat.

"Thanks for the coffee!" shouted Dave.

"Grab the gear!" shouted Rob.

"Get the line! Get the line!" shouted Trevor.

Dave started throwing all their gear into the aluminum boat, bashing and smashing it all. Trevor was trying to get the boat launched and had thrown the wooden oars against the hull with a bang, then he started shouting, "I can't get this $%&* knot undone Dave! How many times do I have to tell you? Use a bowline!"

By this time, Rob had jumped into the boat and had the engine down. He pulled on the starter cord and the engine went, VROOOOM! "Let's GO, Let's GO!" he shouted.

Meanwhile, Quint, Tom, Jim, and I watched all the commotion with mild amusement. They couldn't have made more noise if they were a city.

Tom quietly said, "This is like watching Larry, Curly, and Moe."

"Yup," Quint agreed. Jim and I nodded, fascinated by the show the three were putting on. "Guess we know why they haven't seen any moose in three days."

Rob was on the engine, Trevor was in the middle getting his gun ready, and Dave pushed them off and jumped into the bow.

Just then, two more moose emerged from the treeline. Rutting season had just ended, so the bulls were back to being buddies again instead of mortal enemies. The two newcomers were even bigger than the first one. In fact, the second moose could very well have been a record-setter.

"LOOK!" yelled Dave, and the two others stopped what they were doing. It was like passing through the eye of a storm: it got very quiet and still for a moment.

An eagle circled high above.

Then Rob screamed, "GO! GO! GO!" and the commotion began anew. Could they have been Canadian city dwellers on their first hunt?

The biggest bull startled. He turned and walked back in the woods, sensing bad news on the way. His buddy was hot behind, and in a flash the two huge animals had simply vanished, like some magical woodland creatures.

Rob had his gun trained on the woods, but there was nothing to shoot—until the first moose decided it was time to get out of Dodge. It rose awkwardly on its long legs, but no sooner did it have its feet, then Rob blasted it back down.

"Well I'll be . . ." said Tom. "He got it." He shook his head in wonder.

"Let's go have a look," said Jim.

We motored across the bay in our two canoes. The antlers had a 49-inch spread, which confirmed that the bigger one that got away would have been one for the record books. No one from our hunting party could believe that those three could possibly have bagged a moose, much less a big one like that.

Note to self: sometimes hunting is a skill, sometimes it's just plain, dumb luck.

At the end of the week, a floatplane touched down on the smooth lake, leaving a long V behind as it skated over the water and then taxied to the dock. The pilot, a woman in her 40s, said hello and looked at all that we'd amassed on the dock, including the 14-foot Crestliner and the 25-horsepower engine.

"Gee, is that all?" she asked sarcastically.

Tom gave her a sharp look, smiled, and said, "At least we left the piano behind." *Must be a pilot thing.*

Laughing, I explained to her that the engine was kaput, "Do you think we can get you to fly the boat and engine out along with the meat?"

"How many pounds of meat do you have?" she asked. I told her. Then she said, "Get on the other end of this," indicating that I should pick up the bow of the boat while she picked up the stern. I did as instructed. "Hm . . ." she muttered as she estimated the weight and then we set the boat back down. "And this," she nodded to the engine. Again, we picked up the engine and she estimated the weight. Then she took a notebook and pencil from her pocket and did some calculations. We were all holding our breath as she scribbled.

"Yup. But I can't take a passenger."

I let my breath out with relief and said, "That's no problem. We can take the canoes and meet you in Ear Falls. Can we help you load this?"

"Absolutely," she said.

We loaded the boat on the pontoon and then secured it tighter than Fat Man and Little Boy. She had straps and ropes everywhere, then—she grabbed a roll of duct tape just for good measure.

● ● ● ●

21 • RISK

GUN SAFETY AND GUNS' SAFETIES are important if you don't want to get shot by accident. It really doesn't take much of a mistake to end up with dire consequences. Happily, I've never accidentally shot anyone, or been shot by anyone. Well, once I took a shotgun BB to the back of my head that barely drew blood. I have, however, been caught with my pants down.

I had just finished eating a can of sardines for lunch and was leaning back against a log on a bright sunny day. I sat above a lovely meadow looking down on a couple of beaver ponds, one to the left and another to the right. As I sat enjoying nature, I suddenly felt nature call, so I stood to relieve myself on a nearby log. I was halfway through my business when at that moment, a cow elk appeared. She was walking rapidly down the hill toward the ponds, followed by a delicious-looking 5x5 bull elk.

I dove to hide behind the log I'd just been peeing on and didn't have time to finish things off properly. The cow stopped between the two ponds, in full view and range, but the bull stopped behind a pine tree and I could barely see him, much less get a good shot at him. I positioned my rifle on the log and prepared to take a shot. In my eagerness, I had my finger on the trigger as I pushed the safety, and to my utter astonishment, accidently touched off a round.

BOOM!

And suddenly the quiet, peaceful pond became a great, 10-foot high water fountain! It was spectacular! Better than Vegas! The cow elk jumped out of her skin and ran for cover, and the bull, well, he was a very clever beast. He turned 90° and ran straight away from me, keeping that pine tree between me and him the whole time. I couldn't get another shot off, and both elk got away. I knelt there behind the log, with my pants around my knees, watching the water on the pond settle back down again, and had to just shake my head.

Note to self: never have your finger on the trigger while deactivating the safety.

My son, Troy, and I were with my buddy Skip and his 12-year-old son, Randy. Skip had a .22 Stoeger pistol that he was ripping up the targets with.

We all took our shots, and then Skip and I gave the boys the go-ahead to walk onto the range to collect the targets and put up fresh ones. They were about half-way to the targets when Skip set his .22 down on the table. Unfortunately, he failed to unload it. When he laid it down, it went fully automatic.

The bullets whizzed past the boys' heads and they both dropped like the dead. Skip grabbed the gun, and it was over just that fast.

I felt the Earth spin and I couldn't breathe. It was like someone sucker-punched me. Then, Troy sat up and Randy cautiously peeked over his shoulder.

Skip uttered an incoherent, "Hu . . ." and his knees buckled a little. His face was ashen.

"Thank you, Jesus," I whispered.

Note to self: if you're not using your gun, don't have one in the chamber.

Another close call came when my friend, Larry, and I were

duck and goose hunting on Sioux Lake one year, with my dog, Margo. The three of us were in my 14-foot aluminum boat with a camouflage blind set up around it. Because we were hunting both types of birds, Larry had two guns with him: one 12-gage and one 10-gage Browning pump shotgun. The BPS was laying behind him to the side of the gunwale with the muzzle pointed forward. It has a top-slide safety that needs to slide forward to the on position. It was the weirdest thing, but when Margo tried to get out of the boat to retrieve the duck, she somehow slid the top safety off and pulled the trigger all in one motion.

She shot a dinner-plate sized hole in the camo blind—right beside Larry. We stared at each other with our mouths hanging open for a long time.

Note to self: if you're not using your gun, don't have one in the chamber. Wait! Didn't I already make that note to myself somewhere?

Another note to self: some lessons you just have to learn twice.

I've learned a lot of lessons about gun handling over the years. Another came when I was in Spruce creek. I spotted a nice eight-point buck running along the other side of the creek. I stopped and took the shot. BOOM! The buck collapsed in a heap in some tall grass. Just as I was congratulating myself, I realized the creek was too deep for my boots.

I looked around for a log long enough to span the creek and found a poplar suitable for the purpose. Then I found a couple of sticks for balance as I tight-walked across the creek, leaving my gun behind. I got about half-way across when the dead buck miraculously came back to life and bolted into the woods! I back-tracked across the poplar as fast as I could but by the time I had my gun, it was too late to get off a shot.

I crossed the creek to where I'd dropped the deer and there on the ground was a piece of the antler that I'd shot off. The bullet just grazed his skull. I still have that single piece of antler hanging on my mantle as a reminder to keep my gun handy until gutting my deer.

I was on another hunting trip in the Boundary Waters Canoe Area Wilderness in northern Minnesota with my buddies Larry, Guy, Brandon, and Vern. I brought a Browning automatic rifle with me for the trip, which I'd tested out thoroughly before leaving. We put two canoes in at Lake One and paddled (no engines allowed) through Lakes Two, Three, Four, Hudson Lake, Lake Insula, and finally to Hope Lake. We made it to Lake Insula the first day with the plan to canoe into Hope Lake and call some bull moose in the next few days.

Late that night, an evil wind kicked up and blew the lake into a fury and the trees into a panic—then came a great crash! We leapt from our tents to see that a tree, about 1½ feet in diameter, had fallen a mere three feet from Larry's tent! Even in the dark I could see that his face had turned pale from the close call.

The next morning, we set off for Hope Lake. Brandon was on the paddle, and I had the bow. At a wide spot in the river, we used a cow call. This device is a like a small megaphone that you use to imitate the "broadcast call" of a cow. After moaning and groaning into the cow call, we waited for about 45 minutes, but nothing showed up.

Fine. We decided to move on to a new location, but as we were paddling away, we spotted a bull moose standing about 10 feet back from the lake. We paddled closer and closer to it and I quietly raised my rifle and sighted. I didn't have a great shot because he was facing me head-on. My fear was that he might jump, so I planned to take a brisket shot and then when he turned, I'd get in a double-lung shot.

Closer . . . closer . . . BOOM! I hit him!

As predicted, he quickly turned, and I aimed at the lungs and pulled the trigger and—quick as a flash—nothing happened! The gun jammed! I got my fingers into it and tried to pry out the spent shell, but it was jammed in there hard. As I clawed at the shell, the moose ran into the bush and disappeared.

Finally, I managed to force the shell to eject. Brandon had us up on the beach, and we jumped off the bow of the boat onto shore. We tracked the blood trail until it was dark, but we never did find the animal, dead or alive. The next day we returned and followed the trail again, but to no avail. The moose was gone, and there wouldn't be another one for the rest of that trip.

I was so POed at that gun, I thought about wrapping it around a tree. Before the trip I tested the gun out with three different clips and every one of them functioned with no problems at all. The thing fired perfectly, except when there was a moose in front of it.

Note to self: never go big game hunting with an automatic rifle. This wasn't a lesson I had to learn twice.

● ● ● ●

22 • SWAPPING STORIES WITH CLAUS

FOR ALL THE RISKS INVOLVED in fishing and hunting, driving to and from the sites can sometimes be the most dangerous of all. I've had a few close calls, but one of the worst travel catastophes actually happened to my cousin. He nearly drowned in his own vehicle.

I had stopped in at my uncle Claus's home in Saskatchewan on one of my trips, and we got talking about driving on the logging roads. You have to be very careful on those roads. There's not a lot of traffic on them, but the traffic that does travel on them tends to be big trucks with limited stopping ability as they barrel along carrying huge loads of logs. Also, you can come across washed-out parts of the road with no warning. If you get into trouble, it can take days for anyone to come along. Anyhow, Claus and I were jawing about the dangers when he told me a story about his own son, Fred.

Fred was a road grader for a logging operation back in 1979.

"Fred's job was to keep the roads across land and lakes open for the logging trucks," said Claus. "One day, he was grading the road over Lake Athabasca, in Northern Saskatchewan, when the grader broke through the ice. He couldn't escape before it dropped into the ice water and he was dragged to the bottom."

I shifted uncomfortably. Was Claus telling me the story of how his son died? I knew he had a son, but I had never actually met the man. What a horrible way to go! Drowning inside your vehicle in ice water!

"He was underwater when he finally escaped and kicked to the surface. I guess he came up right under the ice at first. By the grace of God, he just happened to turn in the right direction to find the hole in the ice where the grader fell through. He swallowed a lot of water, but he could breathe," said Claus. I let out the breath I'd been holding. He lived!

"He wasn't far from hypothermia, though. He clawed back on top of the ice and tried to run to the road, but his clothes started to freeze. It was minus 30 Celsius—about minus 22 Fahrenheit to you Americans. Damn cold in any language. He was able to walk a mile and a half to shore, and then stumbled another half-mile down the road before he froze solid and couldn't move." Claus was visibly shaken by the telling of the story. Had Fred survived drowning only to succumb to hypothermia?

"Well, by God, it wasn't long before two guys came by in a pickup truck and found him, near to dead. Fred was so frozen that they could not bend him enough to get him into the cab of the truck!" said Fred.

"You're kidding?" I cried.

"Nope," said Claus. "At minus 30, water freezes fast. Anyone who lives in the north knows about hypothermia. It doesn't take long to die. So, these guys in the truck knew enough to just put him in the pickup box and drive as fast as they could to the nearest shelter. When they got to the logging camp, they hoisted him into the bunkhouse and then slowly and carefully warmed him up."

I nodded and said, "I've heard that you don't want to warm someone with hypothermia too fast."

"That's right," said Claus. "You can put the person into shock and kill him faster than the cold would have."

"So, is Fred okay now?" I asked.

"Oh sure. He lived through the ordeal. He lost an ear and some skin on his wrist," Clause flicked his own ear and indicated an area on his wrist. "In fact, he went back to work the next day. Although," he added with a wink, "he did transfer out to another camp a week later."

I said, "I imagine he'll think twice before driving a road grader across ice again."

Claus nodded and said, "Yes, well, I certainly hope so," and offered me another cookie.

"Hey Claus," I said to my uncle between bites of cookie, "Did you ever know my dad's cousin, Rudy?"

"Oh sure," he said.

"Well Rudy taught me how to shoot pheasants from the car."

"Is that so?" Claus encouraged.

"We'd drive along a road with a weedy ditch and watch for the ring around the rooster's neck. Then, we'd drive about 60 feet past it and stop. We'd get out, but because we were far enough away, the rooster didn't spook, and Rudy could shoot it."

"Yup, that's a good technique. I've used it myself a time or two," said Claus.

"I taught it to my buddy Ken once," I said.

"Oh yeah?" said Claus.

"Well, Ken had just got his driver's license and we decided to take his dad's '54 Plymouth sedan hunting for pheasant on our own. Ken spotted a couple of nice roosters in the ditch, drove past about 60 feet, and I got out and Akansased two of them with one shot!" I held up two fingers like a victory sign.

"Good one!" laughed Claus.

"Took me another 50 years to do that again," I said.

"Not an easy job," he agreed.

"Nope. So anyway, we got back to the house and I showed Ma my catch—I was so proud of myself—and she said, 'you catch 'em, you clean 'em.'"

Claus chuckled at that and said, "If I remember right, Rudy used to get your mom to clean about three birds a day?"

"Yeah," I said. "I guess I can't really blame her for not wanting to carry on with that tradition for another generation."

"No," smiled Claus.

"Prob'ly didn't help that she was in her Sunday best at the time and had her ladies over for coffee."

"HAH! No—prob'ly not! Poor timing!"

"So, Ken and I cleaned the birds, but when it came time to go, his dad's Plymouth wouldn't start," I said.

"Dead battery?" asked Claus.

"No, the battery turned over, it just made that 'grr, grr, grr' sound."

"Out of gas then?"

"I asked Ken that, but he said there was an eighth of a tank still. We looked under the hood but couldn't see anything obviously wrong. We kept at it for so long that we killed the battery."

"Uh oh."

"Yeah. So Ken's getting pretty worried by now. That car was his dad's brand-new pride and joy. His dad laid it on really thick about how letting Ken drive the new car was a privilege and big responsibility."

Claus nodded his head with understanding, then shook it with commiseration.

"So, I told Ken, 'I'll get the John Deere B and some rope. We'll bump start it.'"

"That might have worked if the only problem was the battery, but it wasn't," Claus pointed out.

"We didn't think of that at the time. I just tied 'er on and pulled that car around the yard until I didn't have to mow the grass!"

Claus laughed at the mental picture of me sitting on a tractor crushing Mom's grass under the big wheels, the Plymouth skidding out every time Ken popped the clutch.

"Finally, the only thing I could think to do was to crawl under the car. It was the only place we hadn't looked at yet. So, I get under there couldn't believe what I saw!"

"What?" demanded Claus.

Laughing, I said, "The gas tank looked like a crushed soda can! The fuel pump had sucked so hard that it sucked the air right out of the tank! He wasn't just out of gas, he was out of *fumes!*"

"HAH!" cried Claus, "I KNEW it! I knew it was the gas! Didn't I say?"

"The fuel gage was faulty!"

"I knew it had to be the gas!" Claus was very pleased with his detective work. "So, how did Ken's dad take the news?"

"He didn't," I said. "I don't think Ken ever told him."

"Well, he must have wondered why it suddenly cost him a lot less to fill the tank, or why he wasn't getting as many miles to the fill."

"You'd think, but he never said anything. I don't know if he ever noticed it or not. What I *do* know, is that Ken never, ever, to this day, lets his gas tank go below an eighth of a tank!"

● ● ● ●

23 • CAPTAIN DIEHARD

GENEROSITY OF SPIRIT IS A quality that many of my friends have. So many of them have shared the location of their best fishing hole with me or brought me with them to their favorite hunting grounds. I'm blessed to have that kindness in my life. So when my friend Jim called me up and asked if I wanted to join him and two others on a salmon-fishing trip on Lake Michigan, I was happy. I was keen to try fishing on the Great Lakes.

Jim was the same good friend I'd been fishing and hunting with at the Chute. Although he'd hit a rock with our engine on that trip, so did I. It was with great enthusiasm that I agreed to meet him. I drove due east from my home in Hutchinson, Minnesota, for about eight hours, to Algoma, Wisconsin. I slept in a hotel that night and was up early to meet Jim at the marina. We heartily shook hands.

"Good to see you, Jim," I said.

"Good to see you too, Gary." He turned to introduce me to his other two buddies, Sam and Richard. "Let's go and meet our captain, he's already on the boat."

"Which is ours?" I asked. Jim pointed out a 40-foot, white boat with a fly-bridge. Looked good to me. I followed the other three guys down the dock to the boat where they introduced the skipper, Clark Coburn.

"Welcome aboard!" Clark boomed. He was an average-looking

guy, of average height and build, maybe in his late thirties. His front teeth were a little proud, but he had a firm handshake. He showed me where I could stow my things and we were soon underway.

"So, Clark, how long have you been doing this?" I asked as we flew across the surface of the lake.

"About eight years now," he said. "Not to brag, but you're lucky to get me as your skipper today. I've got a *solid* record for bringing in the biggest and the most fish out of all the skippers in all the charter companies." He went on, "Last year I had the record for not one, not two, but for the *three* biggest fish of the year. Just last month I brought a group of guys out from Chicago, and I took them to one of the best places I know—I'm taking you guys there now—and I came back with more fish than the coolers could hold. There was another skipper—one of my competitors—on the dock when we came in, and he couldn't believe it. I said to him, 'Oh yeah! Believe it baby!' I mean, don't get me wrong, he's a good guy and all, I guess I just have more luck than him, maybe I just know the better places."

"Is that right?" I said politely. Privately, I thought, *Someone, please change the channel.*

He continued, "I don't want to get greedy though, you know? I mean, there are a lot of good fishermen out there, and I guess I should leave a few fish in the lake for them too!" He laughed at his own joke.

Jim asked, "So where are we going today?"

"I'm taking you to a little hole I know where the salmon are thick. Not only are there lots of them, but they're big!" said Clark. "This is the place where I caught the second biggest fish last year."

Jim said, "Sounds good. I'd like to get a big one."

"*One?*" cried Clark. "No, no, no. You don't want just one.

Today, you want at least two big ones. Two big ones will satisfy *me* today."

"Okay, two big ones then," said Jim, giving me a look.

Soon, Captain Clark slowed the boat down and we set to the business of putting the lines out. To his credit, while trolling, he managed to set up eight lines and not tangle them. He put out four lines on downriggers (a device to get your fish hook down deep), and then another four surface lines.

Once the lines were out, there wasn't much left to do.

The four of us paying customers drew cards to see who would get to reel in the first fish that hit. Sam pulled the high card, so he had first dibs, then me, then Jim, then Richard. It was a pleasant enough day as we slowly motored along. The sky was blue, the water was flat calm, and there was a little bit of lake fog making for a very picturesque morning. I sipped serenely on my tea while we all waited for one of the eight rods to twitch. It was good tea. Yup. I put some honey in it. I think it was from Sri Lanka—the tea, not the honey. Waiting.

Finally, Sam detected the slightest tug on the tip of one of the poles with its line attached to a downrigger. "Fish on!" he called. Then he grabbed the pole, reeled the line in a little and dropped the tip close to the water, then quickly yanked it up so that the line would separate itself from the clip holding it to the downrigger. With the line freed, he could reel the salmon in, letting line out or reeling it in, depending on how the fish responded. It wasn't long before Sam landed a rather small salmon.

I caught the next one, also small, so Jim was up next. Eventually, after a wait that seemed longer than a Billy Graham invitation to receive Jesus, we heard the cry, "Fish on!" Jim grabbed the pole, dropped the tip, and yanked it back. The line snapped free from the downrigger and the fight was on. This was clearly a big fish. It took great lengths of line before slowing enough so that Jim could reel some back in. Then it would dive again, and Jim would have to give it more line. Back and forth, back and forth, the fight continued.

Then the line went slack. He lost the fish, along with the bait.

"Ohhh, too bad Jim," I said. Sam and Richard made similar comments as we shook our heads at such rotten luck. It happens. But Clark responded differently. He snatched the rod from Jim's hands and reeled the rest of the line in.

"What were you thinking?" he snarled. "You should have just given him the line. It's not like you're paying for it by the foot."

"What?" asked Jim, shocked—as were the rest of us.

Clark, a.k.a. Captain Dudley Diehard, jammed the rod back into its holder and turned on Jim like an angry school teacher. "I said—" and he grabbed Jim by the arm and started shaking him and scolding him like a naughty child, "that you should have let the fish have the line. That's why you lost it!" He was coming completely unglued!

"Get off!" said Jim, slapping Diehard's hand away, but he clung tight and kept shaking.

"I thought you said you know how to fish? You told me you've done lots of fishing," His voice had become shrill, "You should know when to let line out and when to reel in! Even a rookie knows that!"

Jim jerked his arm away from Diehard, breaking the grip he had on his arm, and growled, "Get. Off. Me."

Captain Diehard threw his hands up in mock surrender, "Fine. I just thought you were a fisherman. I can see you're not." Then he turned to Richard and said, "You're up next. Don't blow it like this guy did." With that, he turned heel and stomped up the ladder to the steering station on the fly bridge.

The four of us looked at each other in complete shock. At

some point, I realized my mouth was hanging open, so I closed it. Jim's face was still scarlet. Sam and Richard's eyes were the size of saucers. We all exchanged looks that read, *We're on this boat with a crazy man.*

The silence was broken by the sound of one of the surface rods letting line out. Sam said to Richard very quietly, "Fish on."

The ride back to shore that day did not include a lot of talking. Captain Diehard was still sulking, and we had caught very few fish. It was not fun. Clark had forgotten that the purpose of fishing is to have fun. Somewhere along the way, he lost track of the thrill he must have had that first time he dropped a line in the water and felt the tug of a fish. But what do I know? Maybe he never got to have that thrill. Maybe for Clark, fishing was all about the conquest: win, win, win at all costs. Maybe he had cruel parents who raised him to be a "winner" and as a result he became an angry overachiever who had to win at all costs. Who knows what goes on in the minds of men, but this time he didn't win. This time, he lost a tip and four customers.

Note to self: you can't win 'em all.

● ● ● ●

24 ● ARCTIC LODGE

A COUPLE YEARS AFTER OUR little encounter with the crazy Captain Diehard, Jim invited me along on another fishing trip with him and several others. This time, we were heading to the Arctic Lodge, on Reindeer Lake, Saskatchewan.

With all the tributaries, and the sheer size of the lake, the fishing is amazing. A person can choose what kind of fish to put on the grill that night: northern pike, lake trout, Arctic grayling, or walleye. I chose E: all the above.

We chartered a Douglas DC-4 airplane and flew from Minneapolis, Minnesota. The further north we went, the fewer roads scarred the landscape and the more lakes showed up. By the time we were flying over northern Saskatchewan, the land was completely pockmarked with thousands upon thousands of lakes, which had thousands upon thousands of islands. When I looked down, I saw myself, sitting in a boat, with a fishing rod. Soon I felt the plane bank and spotted an island with a small airstrip below.

"Ladies and gentlemen, this is your captain speaking. We are currently over the Malcom Island Airstrip. Unfortunately, there is a disabled plane on the runway, and they can't clear it right away. We've been redirected to an airstrip near Lynn Lake in Manitoba. From there, a bus will meet you and take you into town where you can enjoy a hot meal. Afterward, we will have the bus bring you back to the airport as soon as we know we can land. We apologize for the inconvenience and thank you again for your patience." With that, the plane headed east.

When we got to that restaurant in Lynn Lake, I could have eaten everything on a pig but the oink. Walking in the door was like walking back in time. It was a '50s café with a long counter and round stools bolted onto the floor on one side of the room. On the other side were tables with bench-seats whose padding was cracked and faded where thousands of people had slid in and out of the booths over the years. Jim, myself, and a few others took seats at the counter. As hungry as I was, the décor had me a little dubious about the fare. If the same care was taken with the food as with the linoleum flooring, we were in trouble.

The furnishings were rough but the waitress was rougher. She was a young blonde woman who glared at all of us fishermen, just arrived off a bus, crowding her space. She was 60 percent tattoo, 30 percent metal appendages, and 10 percent surly obnoxiousness. Raking us with her heavily made-up eyes, she jammed both fists onto her bony hips and said, "Coffee?" To which we all nodded.

Her nametag read, "Terri," and she slammed a cup in front of me and splashed some coffee into it. I took a sip and, despite my fear that it might do permanent damage to my taste buds, I said nothing. Jim took a sip and discreetly spat it back into the cup.

Picking up the menu, I asked Jim, "So, what do you think is safe?"

He looked over the meager menu and shook his head, "Not sure about the liver and onions, and I wouldn't trust the kidney pie to be free of neighborhood cats, but I don't imagine you can go too far wrong with a burger and milkshake in a place like this."

"That sounds about right to me," I agreed, and placed my order.

Our burgers and shakes arrived about 20 minutes later. Terri dropped off our plates from a height as she flew around taking orders, delivering plates, clearing dishes. The milkshakes came soon after, slopping a little as she slammed them down in front of us and ran off to do something else, all the while muttering under her breath.

The burgers on our plates were something else, and truth be told, actually *did* resemble the linoleum. The buns were thin and flat, and we had to lift the top off to make sure there really was anything in between the two pieces of bread. A stingy, gray puck of mystery meat with one blotch of yellow, one blotch of red, and one wilted leaf formed the "burger" part of the meal. The fries were your typical skinny, greasy-diner fries. The milkshake appeared to be devoid of ice-cream. It was more like a cold glass of chocolate milk, thin as broth. Could man survive on this?

"Excuse me, Terri?" said Jim.

Terri was whipping past us when he spoke her name. She snapped her head around and barked, "What?"

"I was just wondering if I could get some ice-cream in my milkshake?"

Instantly, Terri slapped her hand down on the counter in front of Jim, got up in his face and said, "You piss me off!" then stomped away.

Out of the corner of his mouth, Jim said, "She reminds me of Captain Diehard." I snorted a little coffee up my nose and had to sniff it back.

I guess the pressure of serving a few fishermen pushed her over the edge. Along with her temper, she also lost her tip.

We ate, paid, and strolled around the two-horse town for another hour or so before we finally got word to board the bus again. We all piled in, drove, piled out, piled onto the plane, flew, and around 10:00 p.m. we finally piled off the plane and onto the Malcom Island Airstrip. We were so far north that the sun was still relatively high. In fact, even at midnight I could have read a newspaper outside.

Not far from the airstrip, there was an armada of small, aluminum fishing boats waiting to take us and our luggage to the Arctic Lodge. Once more, we piled in and then piled out. Finally, after a long day of travel, we reached our last stop. There was a main lodge and several smaller log cabins, each with a few beds and a wood stove.

The main lodge was beautiful. It was built entirely of logs, with post-and-beam construction, a steep roof, and floor-to-ceiling windows facing the lake. It sported a pool table, poker table, river-rock fireplace, leather furniture, and a dining room where you could watch the water as you ate breakfast and dinner; they served lunch on the lake. Not having had much nourishment at the restaurant in Lynn Lake earlier, we enjoyed a very fine steak dinner and headed to our cabins to rest up for the fish massacre we planned for tomorrow.

Given that the sun never really set, I can't say we were up before "sunrise," but suffice it to say it was early. I gathered up my rods and walked over to the lodge for a quick breakfast. Then they assigned everyone a fishing guide. One by one, fishermen paired off with a Woodland Cree, who are native to Reindeer Lake and are generally known for knowing their business. I, however, was the last one in line and was assigned a 15-year-old newbie. "Lost One" was my name for him. He was still learning his trade and was supposed to follow his dad around the lake, lest he get lost.

For a 15-year-old, Lost One managed to put us into some excellent fishing spots—even if he was staying close to two other boats. First, we trolled for northern lake trout and caught several five-to-ten pounders. Then we switched to Arctic grayling. These were my favorite, despite being much smaller than the trout. Sometimes they're referred to as the *Sailfish of the North* due to their exceptionally large dorsal fin. After lunch, Lost One started poking into shallow reefs and pointed them out when he saw them surface feeding.

"There," said Lost One, pointing to an area where the water was a lighter color. He cut the engine and took up the oars.

Their tall fins stuck up from the water in schools of 50 or more. We quietly floated toward them, taking care not to spook them away. I used an ultra-light rod with #2 or #3 Mepps Spinners. The spinners, when underwater, spin very quickly, simulating the beating of an insect's wings and creating a wing-beating sound. I've used them often and find them to be very effective in situations like this.

Almost immediately after my first cast, I hooked one. It went crazy! What a terrific fight it put up! It jumped and twisted and pulled left, right, left, right. It was all I could do to keep up with it, especially on such light tackle. It was a beautiful fish and a good, sporting fish. I landed that first one, then followed the school that had moved a little distance away because of all the commotion and landed a second one soon after. I even got one that I still have mounted on my wall in Minnesota today.

At about 3:00 p.m., our group of three boats headed back to camp. Lost One was the last one to leave. We were following the others when he said, "I know a shortcut," and he pulled away from the others.

"You sure about this?" I asked.

"Yeah, we'll beat them back," he replied.

I wonder how many misadventures started with the words, "I know a shortcut."

We passed several small islets, then Lost One turned into an inlet. He grinned like the Cheshire cat, he was so pleased with himself. When he realized the inlet was really a small, dead-end bay, the smile faded.

"Oh, I think I turned one too soon," he explained to me. We putted out of the inlet, past a couple more islets and then into another inlet, which was again, a very deceiving dead-end bay. This time, all he said was, "Hunh."

We found two more dead ends before he asked me, "Do you have a map?"

"Why would I have a map? You're the guide," I replied.

"Yeah . . ." he said and looked around at all the islands and all the water and all the places to get lost. "Well, do you have a compass?"

Now I was concerned. "No. You're the guide. Besides, what do you need a compass for? It's a beautiful day and the sun is in the west."

That seemed to brighten him up, "Right!" and he motored in a new direction. We motored for what seemed like a long time. A couple of times I nudged the gas tank with my toe to see how much was left. I had visions of running out of gas, lost among the 5,000 islands of the 140-mile lake, with no food. How long would it take them to find us? Did we have flares? What kind of safety kit was this boat equipped with, anyway? At least we wouldn't have to spend the night in the pitch black with that midnight sun. These were the thoughts that were crowding my mind when we eventually came across a group of Woodland Cree fishermen.

Lost One and the others spoke in their own language, but it was clear what the topic of conversation was. There was enough hand waving and gesturing to make a mosquito surrender. Finally, Lost One pointed us in yet another new direction and sped off. He seemed confident that he knew where he was going, but how confident can a 15-year-old boy be? He had seemed confident about his shortcut too. So, I felt immense relief when the great lodge came into view, sitting proudly on the shore like a promise.

I learned a couple things from that trip. First, always depend on my own navigation. I have twice been lost due to reliance on others, and I don't intend on having a third misadventure. Where I go, there aren't a lot of street signs, and the feminine technique of asking for directions is rarely a choice. Lost One got lucky.

The second "note to self" came after I got back home to Minnesota. We disembarked from the plane, grabbed our bags and gear, and then got the coolers of fish. I could tell that something wasn't right when I lifted the coolers—they felt light. After opening them up, we found that they'd shorted us at least half of the fish we caught! Fortunately, it only took one *very* tense phone call to get the rest of the fish on the next plane out. Always check your stuff before loading it onto the plane.

Lake fishing.

I guess both those lessons comes down to trust. It'd be nice to live in a world where everyone does what they're supposed to do, but it doesn't always happen that way. Sometimes people mess up despite their good intentions, and other times people's intentions are not what you'd like them to be.

● ● ● ●

25 • SPOOKED

I'D BEEN HAVING SO MUCH fun with lake fishing that I decided to buy myself a 22-foot StarCraft with a cuddy cabin. Although I never had any regrets about buying the boat, I did have a moment.

My friend Jim and I launched the boat into Lake Michigan from Port Washington, Wisconsin. It was a small port along an otherwise smooth coastline. It has a man-made breakwater with a lovely, white lighthouse at the end. The water was as smooth as silk. The V of our wake spread for many hundreds of feet behind us as we motored out about five miles east. It was getting later in the morning and the sun was warmish, although it was still a far cry from the searing grip of summer. We were hoping for salmon, so we had the downriggers out and were slowly trolling south, keeping an eye on the depth sounder.

I had a made a tea and was sipping it, with one eye on the depth sounder, one eye on the rods. In the distance, large freighters made their way north and south carrying their cargos to and from Chicago. I didn't have a lot of experience boating on such huge masses of water, so it was kind of neat to watch them pass.

"Fish on!" called Jim, as he took a rod from its holder. It looked like a good one, judging by the way he had to alternate reeling in and letting out line. I put my tea down and grabbed the net as the fish neared the boat. It leapt out of the water about 40 feet away and then dove once more. Finally, it got close enough to scoop with the net. Jim was happy. It was a respectable fish that put up a good fight, and it would feed his family for several tasty, tasty meals.

Once the excitement of landing the fish was over, I turned my attention back to the water, and to my utter surprise, I couldn't see further than 40 feet! Fog had completely engulfed the boat. There was no sky, no horizon, and precious little water still visible. I shivered with a chill, not only because the temperature had suddenly dropped five degrees, but also because it felt like someone had walked across my grave.

I had been snow blind once, years before, and this was somewhat similar. I had a feeling like I was blind, only instead of seeing darkness, I could see only whiteness. Then, from deep in the fog, came the low, distant moan of the lighthouse at Port Washington.

We pulled the lines and downriggers and, using the compass, turned west.

"Jim, watch forward and listen for any sounds," I said. "We're going to go west until we get into about 50 feet of water, then I'll take us back north. Hopefully we'll find the port without hitting anything."

"Sounds like a good plan," said Jim.

The Great Lakes have long been known as ship graveyards. One reason for that is because wicked storms can explode out of nowhere, catching sailors completely unprepared. Another reason for this, however, is because advection fog forms very quickly on days just like this, and sailors lose their way and put their ships on rocky shores. Still, I was only five miles from shore and I knew it was due west. *How much trouble can we be in?* I wondered, as the foghorn bawled again.

Using only a compass—there was no GPS in those days—I

steered us back to shore. I maneuvered us slowly, so that if we were to suddenly cross paths with another boat, the impact wouldn't be too great. I thought I had a solid plan and I supposed there wasn't much reason to be overly concerned, but the problem wasn't the actual danger. The problem was more the perceived danger.

In my imagination:

All the white around me is only thickening. I am not heading west. I am heading east, north, south, in circles, but not west. I don't know I'm not heading west because the compass is broken. I am doomed to motor around in circles until there is no more gas and then there, in that place of complete silence, I will drift in the solid wall of white until Davey Jones himself comes to claim my soul and condemn me to an eternity of slavery in the watery depths of hell. His ship is in the form of a cargo ship. I hear its low horn in the distance. To the right, there it is—or is it from the left? Nearby—or is it far away? Then, out of the white, the bow of his great ship is bearing down on me! Its anchor is a huge tooth designed to cleave the flesh from my small boat, from my very bones. The vast, razor-sharp edge of the huge ship's bow severs my StarCraft in two. My only hope is to quickly die with it, before Davey Jones knows I'm gone.

The lighthouse sounded its horn again, this time joined by the horn of a freighter.

Jim and I looked at each other with wide eyes. I could tell that he'd been lost in the same grim trance that I'd just been in.

"Did you hear that?" I asked.

"Yeah. A ship," said Jim.

"How close?"

"I can't tell," he said.

"Let's listen for it again," I said.

"I can't even tell what direction it came from," said Jim.

"I know. The sound is weird in here," I said. Even though we were technically way out in open water, in the great outdoors, where I'd spent so much of my life, it still felt like "in here" to me. We were inside the thick, white walls of lake fog, and it was a terrible, claustrophobic place.

Jim nodded, "I think it might have come from behind us— but that could be wishful thinking. I might have made that up."

"Yeah. I know what you mean. Keep your eyes forward though. I don't want to hit anything we might come across." *Like Davey Jones's ship-of-death.*

Then came the low moan of a cargo ship again, quickly followed by the lighthouse's slightly higher-pitched horn.

"Ship," Jim pointed to our boat's four o'clock.

"Good," I replied. Then another ship's horn sounded.

"Ship!" Jim pointed to our seven o'clock.

"Same ship?" I asked.

"Second ship," he said, staring intensely to where the sound came from.

"How far?" I asked.

"Not sure. Not too close though."

"Okay, keep your eyes forward," I said.

"I'll keep 'em everywhere. There's no telling if a ship might come up behind us, or if we run into one," said Jim.

"Fair enough," I said, and tried to blink the white out of my eyes for the millionth time.

We slowly cruised along, listening to the warnings, trying to determine direction and distance. Then, another sound.

"Hey Jim," I said quietly, "can you hear that?" I slowed the engine and put it into neutral, so it would be quieter, but I didn't dare shut it off out of fear that it might not restart for some reason.

Jim looked forward and opened his mouth slightly, "Yeah. I can." He smiled cautiously and said, "I think it sounds like surf."

"That's what I thought too," I said.

"What's our depth?" he asked.

"Sixty," I said. "I'm going to take her in to fifty and then make our turn north."

Once we were in 50 feet of water, I turned the little boat starboard and watched the depth gage intently. I figured no big ship would be in only 50 feet of water; by staying at a uniform depth, we would also stay a uniform distance from shore; and we should be safe from random rocks or reef at that depth. Those were all fairly safe assumptions—fairly. Hopefully we would not be so far offshore that we would not be able to see the lighthouse's light in the thick fog.

"Okay, watch for the lighthouse now," I said to Jim.

"You got it," he said. I could tell he was also still listening. He had his chin raised and his mouth was open a little in concentration.

If it was nerve wracking in the deep water, chugging along in only 50 feet was even more intense. Before, I worried about getting close to stuff. Now, I *knew* I was close to stuff. Fortunately, we didn't have to go much further when Jim shouted, "There's the light!"

At first, I couldn't see it, but then it flashed again, and it was like I was able to breathe once more, "Yeah!" I shouted back. "Right on!"

With that one little flash of light, all hope was restored. It not only pierced the wall of white that had been blinding me, it broke the grip of fear that had been crushing my chest like a heart attack. I could see. I could breathe. We were okay. Davey Jones would not have us today.

● ● ● ●

26 • LARRY

I'M AN INTROVERT. LIKE MANY other engineers, the My-ers-Briggs Type Indicator pegs me as an INTJ (introversion, intuition, thinking, judgment). I re-energize myself by spend-ing time alone, especially time alone in nature. I love to sit in a boat by myself with a fishing line in the water, contemplating the stillness. However, sometimes people make the mistake of thinking that introverts don't want or need people; there can be nothing further from the truth.

My life has been, and is, filled with wonderful people. My family is a constant source of joy to me, and my many good friends are one of my greatest blessings. I'm grateful for all of them, every single day. I wouldn't be the person I am without my parents, or my wife and children, or my friend Quint, or even some of the people who don't feature so prominently: my old boss, Paul; my uncle, Tilford; or Ginny's old roommate. I feel grateful to them all. Still, some stand out more than others. One of those people is my good friend Larry.

I first met Larry in 1981, when my daughter Dawn was dat-ing Larry's son, Mark. One night—I should say early morning since it was about 3:00 a.m.—I caught Dawn sneaking back into our house. I put her under some heavy pressure until she eventually cracked and told me where she'd been. She copped to being out with Mark. I wasn't impressed with the sneaking about, with the late night, or with the entire situation. Naturally,

I was highly concerned about my 15-year-old daughter and her nocturnal activities. The next day, I called up Mark's father, Larry, and met him at a restaurant. I described to Larry the events of the previous night—er, earlier that morning—and explained to him that I had a strong desire to see my daughter make it through high school without getting pregnant! Larry, although completely unaware of the situation, couldn't have agreed more. Despite being so worried about Dawn, I liked Larry. He seemed like a good guy. In fact, I liked Mark, too, even though I was suspicious about his intentions. About a year later, Dawn and Mark split up, but Larry and I remain friends to this day.

Larry is the kind of guy that things just seem to happen to. He doesn't run around making a lot of noise and carrying on, and yet things . . . just happen to him. I can tell dozens of stories about him.

Like once, how in the mid '60s, he was selling insurance. Back in those days, it was common for insurance agents to dress in a dark suit with a white shirt and dark tie. Dressed in his professional best, Larry knocked on a farmhouse door and a man invited him in. In that era—perhaps a kinder, gentler era, or perhaps just a less fearful, naïve era—it was common to invite a stranger in for a cup of coffee or a bite to eat. On that day, he arrived about noon, just before the midday meal, so the man invited Larry to stay for lunch. He gratefully accepted the offer, removed his shoes, and crossed the threshold.

"It's very kind of you to share your meal with me," he said. "My name is Larry."

The older, confident-looking man, said, "Welcome, welcome! Please, have a seat. I'm George." The two men shook hands, "This here is my wife, Claire."

"Pleased to meet you, Claire," said Larry.

The man pointed to two children already seated at the table, "This is our oldest daughter, Michelle." Larry shook hands with a pretty teenager. "This is our youngest, Chantelle." He shook the hand of the shy and giggling girl, who didn't seem like she'd ever had her hand shaken in such a formal way before and didn't quite know how to do it yet. It made Larry smile.

Claire said, "Larry, please, won't you take a seat?" and she pulled out a chair at the head of the table. Larry was taken aback at having been offered the place of honor. What generous hosts! They all took their seats, and when Claire asked that Larry say a table prayer, he thought it might have been a little strange. However, Larry was a Christian, so he graciously consented and said the prayer. The little family and their guest dug into the plates of beef and potatoes and vegetables.

Soon, there came a knock on the door. George and Claire looked at each other, and she said, "Are you expecting anyone else?"

"No," said George with a furrowed brow, and he went to answer the door.

Larry could not hear much from the foyer while seated at the head of the dinner table, but it wasn't long before George returned with another fellow in tow, hat in hand. "Uh, Claire," said George, "*this* is the new pastor, Pastor Rhymes." Then he said to the pastor, "This is my wife, Claire, my daughters, Michelle and Chantelle. And this is Larry."

The pastor shook hands or nodded to each in turn.

Claire, looking baffled, said, "My goodness, well, let me set another place for you, Pastor Rhymes," and she rose from her chair, looking from the pastor, to Larry, and back to the pastor.

"Mommy?" asked Chantelle, "If that's the pastor, then who's he?" pointing at Larry.

Claire opened her mouth to answer, and then closed it

again. She had no answer and merely looked at Larry with the question in her eyes.

Larry rose from his chair as well. "Oh my. There seems to have been a misunderstanding. I—I'm Larry," and he looked at the family as though that explained anything. "I'm not the pastor," he gestured to Pastor Rhymes, as though there could be any confusion about who he was *not*. Everyone just stared at him, waiting for his explanation to begin making sense. Then, in a rush, he blurted, "I represent the insurance company and was just wondering if you good folks might be interested in safeguarding your property and the futures of you and your children in the event of a tragedy—God forbid."

George's eyes grew huge and he said, "You're an insurance salesman?"

"Um," said Larry, "ya."

A moment of silence passed over everyone as the misunderstanding sank in: eyes wide, mouths open.

Claire broke the silence by saying, "Well I guess I'd best get another setting." Smiling at Larry, she said, "George, you go and fetch another chair for Pastor Rhymes. Girls, you scoot down and make some room." She flapped her hands in *go-fetch*, and *scoot-down* gestures, and went to the china cabinet for more dishes.

The family went into action and within moments everyone had food on their plates and they all enjoyed the meal, laughing off the misunderstanding as a happy accident.

You might think that's the end of the story, and Larry did too, for many years. In fact, it was a story he told on many occasions. Twenty-five years later he was at a house party in Minneapolis, and he told the story to a group of highly amused friends, acquaintances, and a couple of strangers. After the story, one of those strangers, a pretty woman, said, "Hello Larry."

Larry thought the woman might have looked a little familiar to him, but he couldn't place her. "I'm sorry, have we met before?" he asked.

"Actually, yes. You don't remember me?"

Larry squinted at her as she smiled from ear to ear, "I'm sorry. You seem really familiar to me, but I can't figure out where we've met."

"Well," she said, "I thought you looked familiar to me too, but I couldn't remember where either, until you told us that story."

"Oh?" said Larry.

"It's me, Michelle," said the woman. "I was the oldest daughter in your story! I was at that table you were just talking about!"

Larry nearly fell off his seat.

And that's the kind of thing that just happens to Larry—all the time. As it turned out, Larry shared the same great love for fishing and hunting as I do. Over the years, we've been on many trips together. I can tell a great many Larry-stories.

One winter, Larry and his dad, George, and I went deer hunting out on an island in Sioux Lake. We set up a big, old army squad tent with a stove on one end and a fireplace on the other. We affectionately called it the *Tiltin' Hilton*. It was so heavy that it was pitch black inside even in broad daylight. It was comfortable too—so comfortable that one morning Larry and George slept through the sunrise well into daylight. In fact, it finally took a gunshot to wake the two of them up (don't ask about the gunshot).

Emerging from the *Tiltin' Hilton*, they rubbed their eyes and stretched and yawned and decided to have a bite of breakfast before moseying out to shoot a deer. They cooked the meal, ate it all down, did the dishes, and finally, eventually, two hours late, showed up to their deer stands. Now, the best time to be at a deer stand is at the crack of dawn. This is when the deer move around the most and you have the best chance of seeing one. On that day, Larry got to the stand closer to the crack of noon.

No matter though—he was Larry, and things just happen to Larry. This time, a great big deer wandered by Larry's stand. He took the shot and hit it, but it didn't drop right away. The buck bolted and ran about a half-mile before finally succumbing to the shot. Larry tracked it down but had to tromp through about 15 inches of snow to get there. He gutted the deer and then began the long trek back to camp, dragging the carcass behind him. He said to me later, "I couldn't believe how heavy it was! Even after I gutted it, I felt like I was dragging an ocean liner." Apparently, after about 150 feet of hauling the carcass through snow, he was sweating like pig who knows what's for dinner. Exhausted, he stopped and put the rope down. It was only then that he realized his snow pants had fallen half-way down and wrapped around his knees! He re-fastened his suspenders and suddenly the task of dragging the deer back to camp got much easier.

One winter, Larry and I brought our wives cross-country skiing to Giant's Ridge, near Biwabik, Minnesota. We all caught a chairlift up the first hill. At the top, Larry pushed himself off the seat and skied down the little slope away from the lift. At the bottom, he leaned back a bit and, to his surprise, one of his boots popped off the ski. No matter, he thought, he'd just kick the boot back into the binding and be on his way with the rest of us. When he looked down, however, he found that the toe of the old, brittle boot had broken away from the rest of the boot! The toe of the boot was still firmly affixed to the binding, and his own stockinged toes were left exposed to the great outdoors. The look on his face was priceless! He ended up ski-hop-ski-hopping down the slope, with one ski on the snow and one ski tucked up under his arm.

One year, when we were on the houseboat at Lake of the Woods, Larry used a piece of rope as a makeshift suspender. This earned him the nickname *Lil' Abner* for the rest of the trip.

On that same trip, Larry spent hours making a beautiful tin-pan of lasagna. At suppertime, he pulled it out of the oven with a flourish, and with his oven gloves on, carried it to the table full of hungry, waiting people. He got half-way across the galley and the pan buckled like the Minneapolis I-35W bridge. There was lasagna all over the floor. Larry's expression of shock and disbelief was akin to the losing politician's face on election night. He may have gotten more sympathy from everyone if his face hadn't been so gut-splittingly comical.

Another trip, same galley: Larry decides to open the Cheerios box from the bottom—no one will ever know why. Unbeknownst to him, someone had already opened it from the top. WHOOSH, suddenly there were a zillion little, Honey Nut Cheerios rolling all over the floor. His mouth and eyes made perfect little "Os" just like the Cheerios at his feet. One of the clever wags in the room piped up and asked, "Would you like milk with that?"

If Larry isn't finding things to happen to him, then I, or someone else, will help the happenings along. On one fishing trip, I got the idea to make his fishing net into a tennis racket. I got some electrical tie wraps and stretched the net tight to the hoop. I put the net back into its place on the boat and went to bed. The next day, a bunch of us went out in search of wall-eyes. Larry soon hooked one and reeled it in. Jerome, Larry's brother-in-law, grabbed the net and went to scoop the fish out of the water, but instead, the fish just bounced around on the makeshift tennis racket. Jerome and Larry had to play quite a game of fish-tennis to get the walleye into the boat. The rest of us were laughing so hard they might have heard us in Kenora, 15 miles away. I was pretty proud of myself, and through tears of laughter yelled, "point, set, and match!"

I fully expected retaliation for my little prank. For the rest of the day I waited, but it never came. When I finally called it a night, I crawled into my bunk, only to find that my bed had been short-sheeted, and I had a peanut-butter pillow case. Uncomfortable, to be sure, but I still think I got the upper hand that day!

The same net that I'd converted into a tennis racket came to good use not long later. I was to take the houseboat from Martin Island through Rendezvous Point and tie up near Cross Inlet. Larry and Todd decided to take a small, open boat from Martin Island through a shortcut and meet us at Cross Inlet. They wanted to do some fishing along the way.

It was around dinnertime when someone asked, "Hey, where are Larry and Todd?" We all looked around and realized that they still hadn't arrived. They should have been there hours before.

"I'll go look for them," I volunteered. Taking one of the smaller boats, I motored to where they said they were going to be. I got all the way to the other side of the inlet when I spotted them. There was Larry, paddling the aluminum boat with his fishing net.

"What happened to your engine?" I asked after coming alongside them.

"Aw, yeah, well . . ." began Larry.

Todd piped up since Larry was being less than forthcoming,

"Evil Knievel over here decided he wanted to go really fast in shallow water."

Larry hung his head sheepishly.

"He had the engine gunned, and we were ripping along when we hit a rock," said Todd.

"Yeah, my hand came off the tiller and things got a little out of control," said Larry.

"A little? Yeah, I'd say a little! We hit about four more rocks after that. Larry got thrown into the middle of the boat, and I hit the bow," Todd rubbed his arm where he presumably hit.

"You okay?" I asked.

"Yeah," Todd said reluctantly. "Just a bruise, it'll heal."

"I take it the engine didn't make it, and you didn't bring oars?" I asked.

Larry held up the fishing net paddle and said, "That'd be why I'm using this."

"Resourceful," I said.

"Yeah, I'm a resourceful kind of guy," said Larry wryly.

"Well," I laughed, "You're something anyway."

● ● ● ●

27 ● TO THE HOUSEBOAT

DURING OUR ANNUAL EARLY-JUNE MIGRATION to the houseboat on Lake of the Woods, I like to get there as fast as possible. I want to maximize the fishing time and minimize road time. So, despite pulling a trailer with a small fishing boat, I tend to push things like speed limits—and tires.

One year, we left home at 6:00 a.m., as usual, and drove our normal route from Litchfield, Minnesota, to Sioux Narrows, Ontario. We always stop at Baudette along the way for groceries, any last-minute items, and some chicken. We'd been on the road for about four hours when I had the thought that Larry might be ahead of me. I usually get to Baudette before him, but on this trip, he said he was going to take a different route. *Could it be that with this new route he managed to get ahead of me? Is it possible that I am* behind *Larry?* No, this could not happen. I put the pedal to the metal.

We fairly floated over the roads at 80 miles per hour. They were generally straight and flat with large pools of water in the ditches. Fields flashed by, trees were a blur. I couldn't have Larry getting to Baudette before me. That wouldn't stand. But as fate would have it, I heard a *thud,* and when I looked in the rear-view mirror, I got a snapshot image of a clear, blue sky, and a thousand tiny pieces of black rubber sailing through it. I couldn't have blown that tire better if I'd used dynamite.

I quickly pulled over and jumped out to inspect the damage.

The trailer was sitting on the rim of the blown tire. I grabbed a jack and got the tire changed as fast as possible. This was going to put me behind Larry. I couldn't believe it. When I finally had the tire on, I jumped back in behind the wheel and sped away.

I may have broken the sound barrier getting to Baudette, but there was no way I wanted to be the caboose on that train. We screamed into the Supervalu grocery store, what seemed like only moments after the tire incident. We needed to grab a few things: I'd forgotten to bring bug spray, I wanted enough frozen bread dough to make 32 loaves of bread (the guys liked fresh bread every day), and a few other miscellaneous items. I grabbed a shopping cart and whipped around an aisle—only to catch the wheel of my cart on the corner of a display of Pringles potato chips. Some fool had built a huge pyramid of cans right in the middle of the road! There was a horrific explosion as hundreds of cans came crashing to the floor and rolled around like cockroaches scattering in the light.

What idiot would booby trap a grocery store like that? I wondered.

Still in a hurry, now embarrassed by the ridiculous commotion, I kicked the rest of the cans out of the way and powered over to the checkout. *That'll teach 'em a lesson in display technology that they won't soon forget!*

Every year thereafter, my family teases me for being banned from the Supervalu in Baudette.

After the Great Baudette Supervalu Debacle, we grabbed some chicken at the deli. We were just finishing up when who should pull into the parking lot?

"Larry!" I called as he entered the deli. "What took you so long?" *I can't believe it! I beat him!* "You know," I said to him, "sometimes you drive like an old lady who just got out of rehab."

After the blown-tire incident, I always made sure I had a new or a like-new set of tires. A couple years ago, we were making the annual trip to the Lake of the Woods on June sixth. I remember the date because it was D-Day. I was towing the boat on the trailer and had my friends Terry and Kevin along. The day before, I had replaced the old tires with two new ones. I had no interest in repeating the trip where I looked into the rearview mirror to see tire shrapnel flying through a clear blue sky. No, sir. So, when the steering wheel under my hands started to vibrate and the trailer began a low growl on the pavement, I pulled the rig over as fast as I could.

An inspection of the tires revealed that all the lug nuts on the left side of the trailer were loose. Despite pulling over the instant I sensed trouble, the bolts had already elongated the bolt holes in the rim.

"Oh, man," I said to Terry and Kevin, "this could set us back a half-day!" This wasn't a matter of changing a simple flat tire. This was a bigger deal.

"Well, let's take it off and see about fixing it," said Terry.

I grabbed my tools, but when I put a wrench to the nuts, I found they had jammed so tightly that my only recourse was to remove the hub as well. With Terry and Kevin's help, we took the tire, rim, and hub off as a unit.

I figured the closest town that might be big enough to have a mechanic's shop would be Sauk Center. However, it was 7:00 a.m., so I wasn't sure we'd find a shop open at that hour.

"I don't want to just leave the boat alone on the side of the road while we take the tire into town," I said to Kevin and Terry. "Can one of you guys stay here to guard it?"

Kevin said, "Yeah, I'll stay." It was decided.

The guys helped me detach the trailer from the car, and then Kevin found a comfortable place off the road to sit down and guard the boat from any ne're-do-wells that might happen along.

Terry and I piled into the car and set off. We hadn't gone far, when Terry shouted, "Look!"

"What?" I asked and slowed.

"There!" he said, pointing, "There's a shop with an 'Open' sign!"

I pulled into the parking lot. "I'll bet he has a torch," said Terry optimistically.

The garage was in a large, square brick building. Two bay doors were open to the early-morning fresh air. A tall, slender man wearing blue coveralls had his head under the hood of an old, classic muscle-car.

"Hello?" called Terry.

The man peered around the car's hood and walked toward us. He appeared to be in his sixties. He looked a little bit like my uncle Tilford, and I got a good feeling from him right away.

"Hi there," I said, reaching out to shake his hand, which he took after wiping his on a rag. His name tag said *Ray*.

"What can I do for you this morning?" he asked.

"I'm Gary, and this is Terry," I began, then I explained our situation.

"Yes, I can help you. Or, you can help yourself if you'd like," said Ray. "The torch is here, and the abrasive cut-off saw is over there. Do you know how to use them?"

"Oh sure, no problem," I was impressed by his trust and generosity.

What was impossible to do on the side of the road was simple with the right tools. Terry cut off two stubborn studs quicker than two rabbits doing that thing they do. We then pressed the useless studs from the hub. However, that left only three studs with any thread on them—not enough to make another 350 miles that day, much less get back home again.

"Hey, Ray," I called.

He poked his head around the hood of the car. "Ya?"

"You wouldn't happen to have a stud bolt or two for this hub would ya?" I asked.

Ray walked across the shop, saying, "Let me take a look." He returned to us carrying a rusty cake pan full of miscellaneous nuts and bolts. We rummaged through it, and after a time came up with the perfect bolt.

"Thank you, Jesus!" I shouted. This one little bolt just saved our bacon.

We pounded the bolt into one of the two empty holes. Job done.

"Ray, how much do you want for all of this good, timely help?" I asked.

"Aw," said Ray, wiping his hands on the rag again, "how 'bout five bucks?"

"Well . . ." I rubbed the stubble on my chin and said, "Will you take twenty?"

That brought a grin a mile wide to the kindly gentleman's face and he said, "Gary, you drive a hard bargain." I just love small towns. This garage really did remind me of my uncle Tilford's place in Rose City.

Terry and I hopped into the car and drove back to the boat and Kevin.

"How'd it go?" asked Kevin.

"Couldn't have worked out better if we'd planned it," I said. "Let's put this tire on and get the show back on the road."

Forty-five minutes had passed from the point where I pulled over, to the point of pulling the rig back onto the road. My fears of losing a half-day were over.

As I drove the several hours to the houseboat, my engineer-mind kept going over what might have caused the problem in the first place. Truthfully, I think that when I put the new tires on, I hand tightened the lug nuts, let the trailer down off the jack, and then got distracted before I finished the job with the wheel wrench.

"So, Lug Nuts," said Terry, "what do you think caused that screw up?"

Ah man, I knew I wasn't going to get out of that incident without some pain. "Dunno," I mumbled.

Terry's no dummy, though, "Kevin, I think our friend over here probably didn't tighten the lug nuts when he put that new tire on."

Kevin chimed in, "Well, you know, he's old, and old guys forget things like that."

"Yeah," said Terry, "Ole Lug Nuts must've just forgotten to finish the job."

"Alright, alright," I said, "I just got distracted. It could happen to anyone."

"Sure, sure," Terry said, nodding vigorously.

"Uh huh," agreed Kevin. "Anyone." He winked.

The sarcasm was thicker than northern Manitoba mosquitos. My two buddies spent the rest of the trip referring to me as "Lug Nuts." It's good to have friends—sometimes.

Later that day, we arrived at the houseboat and were sitting on deck sipping some cool beverages when Larry pulled in with his rig. I might have lost a couple of lug nuts and earned a new nickname, but at least I still beat Larry.

That trip, just like every other annual trip to the Lake of the Woods, was a week full of enough laughter to float a boat. We guys were relentless with the teasing, especially when someone did something dumb (except for the lug nuts incident, which was just a distraction, not dumb). Our wives never really understood it. They thought we were being mean and very insensitive, but we thought the over-the-top insults and jabs were hilarious. We all knew it was just for fun and no one took it to heart.

If it's not verbal sparring, it's practical jokes. It's converting fishing nets into tennis rackets; it's short-sheeting and peanut butter pillow cases; it's snipe hunting with a bag and a stick. The goal is to come up with the cleverest, the funniest, and the longest lasting joke—and no matter what, avoid being the butt of said jokes.

For instance, I can clean 400 walleyes and yet if I leave *one* bone in someone's meal, I never hear the end of it.

"Gary, can you pass me the tartar? I'd like some tartar on these bones."

"Lug Nuts! Can I get some fish with these bones?"

"Gary, what's the matter? Your knife dull?

"Gary, you losin' your eyesight?"

But I try to give as good as I get.

"That's not a bone, that's a built-in toothpick."

"Next time I'll cook 'em, but you gotta clean 'em."

"A bone won't hurt your abrasive mouth."

"You know where to catch the boneless fish?"

You'd be amazed at how easy it is to miss something in the galley because of what you might be paying attention to outside the galley window. Once, I looked up to see three bear cubs playing on my kayak while their mother tried and failed to coax them back into the woods. I might have overcooked something on the stove while I enjoyed the view (others might have said "torched" and "lollygagging"). Another time, I was cooking bacon when I looked out the window, directly into the eyes of a black bear! He was standing on the bow of the boat staring at me. I kicked loudly on the door to scare him away, but I also woke a few other boaters by doing so. Apparently bears love bacon too. Can you blame them? I mean, who doesn't love bacon, the candy of meat?

We eat very well when we're aboard.

Lunch:
Fried Breaded Walleye
- Walleye—enough to feed an army
- Unsalted saltine crackers
- Cornmeal
- Lowry's seasoned salt
- Lemon pepper
- Peanut oil

Before leaving for the lake, prepare the batter mixture. Combine saltines, cornmeal, Lowry's, and lemon pepper in blender and blend until a fine powder. Once at the lake, fillet your walleyes. Dredge fillets in prepared mixture. Fry in peanut oil. Recommend side of steamed, dilled, and buttered potatoes, onions, and cabbage.

Appetizers:
Poor Man's Lobster
(Larry's recipe, invented while under duress when he was moose hunting and got stranded on an island without much food.)
- 5-10lb northern pike
- butter

Prepare bed of wood coals in fire pit. Catch a nice northern pike. Remove only the entrails. Lay on coals and bake until flesh flakes. Remove from coals and peel skin off. Melt butter. Dip chunks of pike into butter and enjoy. (Send up a flare an hour after nightfall if no one has come to rescue you yet.)

Evening Meal:
Smoked Meat
Choose any of the following:
• Prime rib
• Pork loin
• Turkey
• Chicken

Smoke it. Eat it. Rest.

My cousin, Gaylord, is the on-board baker. He makes sticky buns with tons of walnuts and brown sugar, which are to die for. His own weight is testament to the quality of his skills in the galley. Gaylord is one of the regulars on the houseboat nearly every year. He loves to socialize and he's a hard-core fisherman. One day, we left the main houseboat tied to shore, and Gaylord, my elderly neighbor, Elmer, and I took my small fishing boat out. It was a miserable day. The wind was kicking up waves, and the sky was spitting snow. No matter, real fishermen can endure! We hit at least a half-dozen spots over three hours with not one walleye to show for our suffering. Well, at least we could say we gave it everything we had. We finally conceded defeat and returned to the houseboat—only to find that all the other guys had caught their limits right off the back of the houseboat, with all the comforts of home.

Note to self: my suffering does not make fish bite.

Sometime in the early '90s, Gaylord, Elmer, and I went out fishing—as we do. We took my *Death Boat*, as Gaylord dubbed it. It was a modified-V, 16-foot, Jon boat with a 35-horsepower Evinrude outboard. That is to say, it went faster than stink. We were skimming atop the water down the channel between a couple of islands when we came to an abrupt halt. When

I say "abrupt" I don't mean that we quickly slowed down; I mean that we went from 20 miles-per-hour to zero, zip, nada, nothing. I managed to hit a rock the size of a kitchen table. All three of us were thrown forward. I ended up in the middle of the boat, Elmer landed in the bow on Gaylord's leg, and poor Gaylord went completely overboard, except for a leg. The 70-year-old Elmer had a death grip on that leg, trying not to let Gaylord slip away. For his part, Gaylord was bobbing around like a buoy in a category-four hurricane, sputtering and spitting water, flapping his arms about, desperately trying to keep his mouth and nose above water despite having his leg hung up higher than his head.

"Hold him, Elmer!" I called, as I picked myself up off the bottom of the boat.

"I got him! I got him!" shouted Elmer. He was a pit bull on a hambone.

After I managed to untangle myself, my first thought was to help Elmer get Gaylord back into the boat. I climbed forward, but as I did, our combined weight in the bow caused the stern of the boat to lift out of the water. The engine, which I'd left running, started screaming. In the turmoil of the crash, I had forgotten to shut the engine off! So now, the front of the boat is lower, which is helping Gaylord keep his head above water, but the engine is screaming. I had to go back and shut it off. When I moved astern, the bow came up again and forced Gaylord's head back under. It was like an exercise in levers. He got a good gulp of water before I shut everything down and could return to the front of the boat. Meanwhile, Elmer clung to Gaylord's leg like a burr in fur.

I reached over the side of the boat and grabbed Gaylord's belt, but when I pulled, the side of the boat dropped and scooped up a lot of water. Gaylord weighed over three bills; this would not be easy.

"Elmer, let go of his leg and move to the other side of the boat," I thought maybe a counterweight would help, but when I pulled on Gaylord's belt again, it just gave Elmer a teeter-totter ride and we scooped more water into the boat.

Elmer said to me, "What if you and I stay on this side and Gaylord pulls himself in?"

I nodded and said to Gaylord, "Did you hear that?"

"Pfaw! Y—Yuh!" spat Gaylord. His eyes were huge.

I let go and helped him get his leg out of the boat and moved over to Elmer's side. Gaylord grabbed the side of the boat and tried to haul himself in but couldn't do it. We kept scooping up water and I feared we'd all capsize if we kept it up.

"Okay, okay, wait!" I said. "Gaylord, I'm gonna get you over to that rock," I pointed.

"Yup, good idea," he agreed. I paddled the boat and we slowly got Gaylord to the rock. I stopped and let Gaylord get his footing.

"Hey! I think I can stick the bow in between these two rocks," said Gaylord.

I couldn't see which rocks he was talking about, but then if I had a talent for seeing rocks, none of us would have been in that mess. "Okay, give it a try," I said.

He managed to wedge the bow of the boat between the kitchen-table rock I'd hit, and another, slightly deeper rock beside it. Then, he floated/climbed onto the kitchen-table rock. Carefully, with a good grip on the side of the boat, he stood up.

"Good, good!" said Elmer, "Keep coming, we gotcha!"

I wasn't sure I was in complete agreement with Elmer's assertion that we had him; if he were to fall, there was nothing we could do from inside the boat, but I liked his enthusiasm. "Yeah, come on Gaylord, we gotcha!"

"Alright, here goes," said Gaylord. He held the side of the

boat with both hands and swung a leg into the boat. This was the critical point. Would the boat hold? Would it slip away, thus destroying Gaylord's private parts?

The boat seemed stable enough to try the second leg. Elmer and I had him by the arms.

"Ready?" said Gaylord, looking first to me, then to Elmer. "You got me?"

"Yes, yes," replied Elmer. I nodded vigorously.

"Okay. One. Two. THREE!" and he gave a mighty kick off the kitchen-table rock and threw himself over the gunwale. We held onto him for dear life, fearing that his forward momentum might send him headlong over the other side of the boat, but he caught himself and stopped with a thud. For a moment, he simply sat there in the bottom of the boat, in about four inches of water, and grinned. Then he looked up and said, "Well that was thirst-quenching."

We all laughed and slapped each other's backs, with a lot of "Attaboy!" and "Good job!" I started the engine and asked Gaylord and Elmer to join me at the stern. This allowed the bow of the boat to rise out from between the two rocks. I put the engine in reverse and floated away. As we got underway, I noticed that Gaylord was shaking like a trailer in an F-4 tornado.

We returned to the mothership for dry clothes and hot coffee. Gaylord and I decided to get back out fishing. We worked hard and didn't have one fish to show for it. Elmer, on the other hand, had enough excitement for one day and decided to hang out on the houseboat. I was impressed with Gaylord. That was quite an experience he'd been through. I'm not sure I would have had the gumption to get back on the horse like that, but he was a true cow-buoy.

● ● ● ●

28 • LAKE MICHIGAN TROUBLES

JIM TOWED A 22-FOOT FIBERGLASS boat from Florida to Minnesota and was itching to try it out on the Great Lake waters, so in early April we made a plan. Jim and Dick would haul the boat behind Jim's motorhome from Minneapolis, to Wisconsin. Larry and I would fly over in Larry's Mooney airplane and meet them at the marina in Rowley's Bay.

The flight that morning was uneventful and beautiful. We soared over city, town, and country, through pristine, cold, early April air. As we approached Lake Michigan, the water was a beautiful deep blue, with emerald green that lined seemingly endless shores. That is one big lake! A half-hour after we touched down, we met Jim and Dick at the landing at Rowley's Bay. They arrived the day before and had Jim's nice, new-to-him 22-foot salt-water boat in the water and ready to go.

Larry and I took the seats at the back of the boat, Dick and Jim sat forward, with Jim on the wheel. "Jim, where're we going?" I asked once the four of us were on board and on our way.

"I thought we'd head back to that spot we caught all that trout the last time you and I were out," he said.

"That sounds good," I agreed. It didn't take long to get there, it was only about eight miles away. As we approached the area, however, the engine died on us.

"What the . . ." muttered Jim as he turned the key several times. Turning the key had nearly no effect. There was a clicking sound, indicating that there was power, but nothing turned over.

"Let me have a look," said Larry, and he removed the cowling from the engine. After poking and prodding for a while he sat back on his haunches and said, "Hunh."

"Let me have a look," said Dick, who swapped seats with Larry and did some of his own inspection work. After some tinkering he gave up and said, "Hmmm."

"Lemme look," I said, and poked around in the engine too. After a time, I could see that there was nothing for it. It had seized and that was that. I sat back, looked at Jim with regret, and said, "Humph."

"Well—" said Jim, "Let me look." Jim and I switched seats and Jim poked at the kaput hunk of engine hanging uselessly off the transom.

After this grim round of musical chairs, Jim finally declared, "It's dead."

We all nodded our agreement, casting our eyes about for a passing boat to flag down as we bobbed helplessly in the water, about a mile from shore.

I said, "Too much salt water and not enough maintenance."

"Looks that way," Jim agreed.

We floated for a while until we spotted a boat in the distance, heading our way. We all four stood up and waved them over. The boat veered in our direction.

"Ahoy!" called the captain. There were two men in a 25-foot Sea Ray powerboat with nearly a half-dozen rods perched on top.

"Ahoy!" called Jim. "Can you give us a hand?"

"Grab the line," said the captain as his buddy put out a couple of fenders and threw us a line. We pulled them in and tied alongside.

"So, what's the problem?" asked the skipper.

"The engine seized, we're going to need a tow. Any chance you can take us back to the Rowley's Bay landing?" asked Jim.

The skipper looked us over and then zeroed in on Dick. He narrowed his eyes and said to his buddy, "I don't know Ben, what do you think? This guy looks like he's a Viking's fan." He pointed out Dick's purple and gold shirt.

"A Viking's fan?" Ben said, aghast. "I don't know about towing any stinkin' Viking's fans." Ben was wearing the green and gold of the Green Bay Packers football team.

Just our luck—saved by Packers Backers—Cheeseheads! There would be no dignity in this rescue.

"Well," said the skipper, "we might consider giving you a tow if you admit who the better team is." He raised an eyebrow.

Together, as though we had rehearsed it, the four of us shouted, "Vikings!"

"OH! Wrong answer! Ben! Cut that line!" laughed the skipper.

"Wait!" shouted Dick. There was a moment where both sides fell silent, then Dick said solemnly, "I was at both games where the Packers beat the Vikings last year, and I will confess, you were the better team in 1984." Truth be told, they hammered us: 45-17 in the first game, 38-14 in the second.

The skipper grinned from ear to ear and said to Ben, "What do you think? Should we give these guys a hand?"

Ben replied, "Aw sure. They're just a bunch of Vikings, lost and helpless on the water. I doubt there will be much pillaging. Let's help 'em out." They were really laying it on thick.

Dick's confession may have saved our waterlogged butts because the skipper reached across the water between our two boats to shake Dick's hand. "Mighty big of you. I'm Lenny, this is Ben."

We made introductions all around and we were soon under tow on our way back to Rowley's Bay. The Packer Backers delivered us safely and then left for their own day of fishing. It was still early.

Jim went to get his GMC motorhome with the trailer and soon arrived at the top of the ramp. While the thin morning sun had melted patches of frost here and there, the steep incline down to the water was still mostly in shade and had thick patches of white. Jim loaded the boat onto the trailer, cinched it up, and shouted, "Okay!" to Dick, who was driving the motorhome. Dick tried to haul the heavy fiberglass boat up the icy ramp, but it was slick, and the RV's tires did a lot of spinning and not a lot of pulling. Soon, blue smoke bellowed out of the vehicle. Inch by precious inch, the motorhome found traction and the rig moved forward—until it hit the next patch of frost, all the while belching blue smoke. The smoke of burned rubber hung in the air like fog. It seemed to take forever to get the boat up onto dry and level land, but they managed it: at what cost, they would find out later.

As it was still early in the day, Larry said to me, "We came this far, we might as well try to rent a boat for the day."

We were of the same mind, so, while Jim and Dick went to see about hiring an outboard mechanic, Larry and I walked to the local hardware/sports store to see what they had to offer. It turned out, they didn't have much. They had one three-horsepower, air-cooled Clinton engine, and a dingy. That was it. My electric razor had more power than that. Really, they shouldn't have even offered us the hunk of junk, and we had no business agreeing to the deal, but they probably had a long hard winter and were desperate for the money, and we'd flown all that way and were desperate to slay some fish. We took it.

No surprise, we had a difficult time starting the old Clinton at the dock, "Maybe it just needs to warm up. It'll probably work better after it's had a chance to run for a while." Wishful thinking. The little engine coughed and spat, heaved blue, left a rainbow streak of oil in the water behind us, and howled like a banshee. If noise were speed, we could have made it to Toronto and back by noon. As it stood, it took Larry and I a half-hour just to get into water deep enough to fish.

We put two lines out and started to troll just as the engine died.

"Are you kidding me?" I asked the engine.

It had no reply.

Reeling my line back in and stowing the rod, I stood in the little dingy and pulled on the Clinton's starting rope.

Nothing.

Again and again, I hauled on that line until I was panting with effort and my arm hurt. That engine Just. Would. Not. Start.

I sat down in defeat, caught my breath, and rotated my rotator cuff. Fortunately, we hadn't gone far from the marina and there were some other boats around. When one came close enough to us, we flagged it down.

"I can't believe it," said Larry as the boat got closer. There, on the skipper's head, was a green and gold trucker's hat. "More Cheeseheads."

After taking a tow back to the dock for the second time before noon that day—by Packer Backers no less—I felt that my dignity had been violated and I wanted to eat something big. Larry and I tracked down Jim and Dick and we found a restaurant where we ordered one of everything. After lunch, they gave us a ride back to the airport.

Considering our luck with machines that day, Larry and I examined every inch of his Mooney. We tested the tightness of every nut, ran fingers over every rivet, checked the levels of every fluid. We scrutinized that airplane like it was the Enola

Gay about to drop Little Boy on Hiroshima. I'm not sure if I should attribute our successful flight back to Litchfield to our impeccable pre-flight probing, or if our bad luck with engines held only for water vehicles, but we made it home safe and sound without further incident.

Jim and Dick, however, did not fare as well. They got 75 miles out of Rowley's Bay when the motorhome started to complain. Jim pulled it over and discovered that they'd compromised the front wheel drive bearings while hauling the boat up that icy ramp. The fix was neither cheap nor fast. They sat in that spot for several days waiting for the parts to show up. Meanwhile, they ate Fish Stix.

● ● ● ●

29 • ALASKA WITH GINNY

THE FIRST TIME I WENT to Alaska was in the summer of 1988. Ginny and I made the trip together. I could hardly believe my eyes when we first flew over. The pristine majesty of the place stole my breath as well as my heart. We flew over hundreds of glaciers and thousands of crystal-clear lakes reflecting azure skies. Trees crowded together in dense, green forests. Rivers cut through them like the veins of a living entity. The forest was vast and absolutely wild. I could not wait to land so I could breathe the immaculate air and touch remnants of the ice-age. And kill fish. I really wanted to kill fish.

We landed in Anchorage and rented a car. First, we drove north, to visit Elmer's step-daughter Cheryl, and Cheryl's husband Jim. They were homesteaders with a place somewhere between Fairbanks and McKinley Park. They lived off the land, by their own sweat and competence. Jim was a teacher and bush pilot, and Cheryl was a cabinetmaker. Her shop was right there on the property, and she was her own boss. She said that some days, especially when Jim would come home POed about something the school principle said or did, being her own boss was the best decision of her life.

When I was a younger man, I often thought about living their kind of lifestyle. I would live off the land, homeschool my kids, chop my own wood, fill my own pantry. Maybe my dreams of living rough stem from having spent my first three years of life on the farm without electricity (I have a dim memory of Ma warning me not to touch the outlet when we first got power to the house). Maybe it came from reading the *Lone Cowboy* too many times. Wherever it came from, it stayed with me. However, living that kind of life would have meant that I'd need to raise chickens, and I just can't stand chickens.

We had a wonderful visit with Jim and Cheryl, but we were also keen to get on with our fishing trip. We drove back down the magnificent Highway #3 where Alaskan eagles were as common as Minnesota mosquitos. Jagged mountains cut the sky like daggers. Rivers raged alongside the road, entirely indifferent to us. We turned south onto Highway #1 and passed back through Anchorage, then down onto the Kenai Peninsula.

Ginny and I had a long time to talk on that drive. One of the many things we discussed was my work. I'd been working for Hutchinson Tech for 10 years by then, and I was feeling like it was time for some change. I'd been working for other people my whole life, but even when I was a kid I always had it in my mind that I'd like to be my own boss.

I remember when I was 12, my ma showed me how to plant, grow, sow, and then sell beans to the neighbors and family. At 10 cents a bag, I made enough money to buy my very first .22 rifle from Uncle Rudy, for six bucks. I never forgot the sense of accomplishment and pride I felt that day. It never really left me.

"What are you thinking?" asked Ginny.

Rubbing my beard, I sighed and said, "Ah, Ginny, I don't know."

Ginny and I had been married for a long time, but even before we had Dawn, she seemed to know what I was thinking, or what I was going to do, before I did. She knew I had something on my mind and shrewdly asked, "What's your best guess?"

I had some ideas but until then, hadn't talked them out. Now I said, "I've got some ideas for a business."

And that was the beginning of what would become Spectralytics.

After one of the nicest, most beautiful and fruitful drives of my life, we arrived at Eagle's Nest Resort, which was right on the Kenai River. It was a very small resort, but it covered the basics. We spent some time fishing the river, and I hooked a 70-pound king salmon (also called a chinook). That might sound like an amazing feat, and granted, it was a big fish—the biggest ever sport-caught was 97.25 pounds—but I think it had already finished spawning and had turned red. It was ready to die. There was no challenge, no sport, in the catch, so I just pulled the hook out, and let him glide on down the river to live out the rest of its numbered days in the waters in which it had been born.

We tried our hand at halibut fishing instead. The largest recorded halibut catch was a 515-pound monster, snagged in Norway, with the runner-up being a 482-pounder from Glacier Bay, Alaska. You sometimes must shoot an Alaskan halibut with a gun before landing it, to protect the people on board from its thrashing. The halibut is a true king among fish. If that didn't satisfy my itch, nothing would. However, to catch one, we would have to find a salt-water fishing boat.

We asked around for a good halibut guide, and several people directed us toward Jamie and Janet Carroll, who ran a small halibut-fishing charter outfit on the coast. They were both recovering alcoholics and Jehovah's Witnesses.

"Why don't you two join us tonight at our AA meeting?" Janet asked Ginny.

"Your . . ." Ginny wasn't sure she'd heard that right.

"Our AA meeting," Janet confirmed.

"But we're not . . ." Ginny trailed off.

"Alcoholics?" Janet said.

"Right. Don't you have to be an alcoholic to attend those meetings?" Ginny asked.

"I suppose in most places you do, but we have a pretty flexible structure at our meeting. We've had lots of guests attend with members who aren't alcoholics. No one will mind you being there, I promise," said Janet. "And nobody will bite you either."

"Well, if you think it would be all right," said Ginny. I don't think I've ever known my wife to turn down a new experience.

"Sure! It'll be a lot more interesting for you guys than sitting around your room all night," said Janet.

Ginny looked to me and I nodded, so she said, "Okay! Where and when do we go?"

That was the first AA meeting that Ginny or I had ever been to. It took a lot of the mystery out of it for me. I guess it's natural to wonder what goes on behind any closed-door meeting, but it was a lot like a small-group prayer meeting: strong coffee, stale donuts, and people doing their best to understand the world around them and be their best selves. Just another day at the office for Christians like Ginny and me.

The next morning, we met Jamie and Janet at their boat. It was a Sea Ray, 32-foot fiberglass boat, with twin 150-horsepower sterndrive (or I/O) engines. The name painted on the side was "Just for the Halibut." It had a comfortable cabin and spacious open deck. I have to say, it was a nice setup. Jamie was there to greet us and help us aboard with our bags. He was a tall, balding man in his late fifties, in good physical condition. He had a friendly face and was very enthusiastic about fishing. He knew a lot about halibut, so I paid attention.

Janet soon came down the dock with an older man behind her. Once they'd boarded, she introduced David, her elderly father. David was a much smaller man. He was wiry and built kind of like Bruce Lee. We all shook hands and exchanged

Pleased to meet you's. David then shot the proverbial starter gun by loudly saying, "Let's go slay fish!" Now *this* was my kind of guy!

With 300 horsepower, we soared over the waves to the fishing spot in no time. We really had to hang on as the boat crashed into wave after wave. It seemed like a big boat when alongside the dock, but out there on the Gulf of Alaska, it was a grain of salt. When we slowed to a halt, it was a relief to stop crashing and relax into the rhythm of the waves. We began to fish.

For the next two hours, we consistently brought up hali's. No one snagged a monster, but there were no chickens either. We all maxed out on our limits and were quite happy with the day.

The wind started to come up, and the waves grew larger. Jamie said, "I think it's time we pull the lines and get back to shore. The wind is picking up and believe me, you don't want to be here when it's windy."

We reeled in the lines and set off. "Gary and Ginny, will you guys keep an eye out for crab traps? The darn things are everywhere, and it's hard to spot them sometimes. Some of these guys will use a black buoy to mark their traps and you can't see them against the water. Others are white, and you can't see them when there are whitecaps like this. It drives me crazy. I wish everyone would just use orange."

We assured him we'd keep our eyes peeled, but he wasn't kidding about how hard they were to see, especially in choppy water like that. I was sitting on a gunwale looking forward when suddenly, a black buoy slid right past me. "Crab trap! Crab trap!" I shouted. "We just drove over a float!"

Jamie wrenched the throttles back, but it was too late. We had caught the trap's line in one of the propellers. He ran back to see what he could see, which wasn't much. The engines were underneath a short swim-platform behind the transom, so it was impossible to see how badly the rope tangled. The black float bobbed behind us as the wind and water pushed us around. We were hung up.

Jamie returned to the helm and picked up the VHF radio and spoke into it, "Vagabond, Vagabond. Just for the Halibut. Just for the Halibut."

After a moment, the radio said, "Just for the Halibut, Vagabond."

Jamie responded, "Vagabond, go channel seven-eight. Over."

"Channel seven-eight. Out."

Jamie changed the channel and said into the radio, "Vagabond, Just for the Halibut."

"Just for the Halibut. Vagabond. What's happening, Jamie?"

"Hey, Rick. Yeah, whereabouts are you?" asked Jamie.

"We're ah . . . we're about five miles southwest of the marina," came the reply.

"Copy that, I'm probably a couple miles south of you. I just caught a crab trap with my propeller. We could be in a situation here. The wind is picking up, and we're looking at three-to-four-foot waves already. I'm going to try to detach the line, but I'd appreciate it if you would stand by on this channel."

"Yeah, no problem. Do you want me to start making my way over to you?" asked Rick.

"Negative. I'm going to do what I can to lose this line. Stand by for five or 10 minutes," said Jamie.

"Okay, you got it buddy," came the reply. "Standing by on channel seven-eight."

"Thanks man, Just for the Halibut, out," and he cradled the receiver. He returned to stern of the boat and reached over, but the line was too far underwater to reach.

"I think you're gonna have to cut it," said David.

"Can't you just reverse the engine and unwrap it?" Ginny asked.

"No," replied Jamie, "We'd risk more damage by doing that. It's best if I can cut the line. David, can you grab the gaff?"

"Yup," said David.

Jamie went back into the cabin and rummaged around a drawer. He pulled out a long filleting knife and a roll of duct tape. Duct tape! We were saved! He and David came together at the stern, and Jamie took the long gaff pole from David and taped the knife to the end of it, creating a spear. Jamie leaned over the transom and pushed the spear down into the water, but no matter how hard he tried, he simply could not reach the line.

"Aarg!" Jamie was frustrated, and the waves were still building. The crab trap line was bar-tight under the load of the 32-foot boat. Everyone aboard was getting knocked around.

"Okay, I have an idea," said David. We gave him our undivided attention. "I'm going to tie a rope around my waist and take the gaff over the side. I'll stand on the swim platform, and you hold me with the rope. From there, I should be able to reach the line and cut it."

Ginny and I looked at him like he had just suggested assisted suicide, but Jamie and Janet seemed to think that it was a great idea. *Are these people nuts?* Before we knew it, the wiry little 75-year-old, five-foot-six man was climbing over the transom onto the swim grid as his son-in-law paid out rope.

"Gimme the gaff, Janet," said David. She passed him the spear and he leaned over—waaaay over and started sawing the line. I held my breath with my mouth hanging open.

Then, suddenly, we drifted free. The jerking motion of the boat stopped and smoothed out as we began to drift. David handed the gaff back to Janet and climbed back aboard.

"Great job, David!" said Jamie, thumping his father-in-law on the back.

We were free, but the boat had slipped sideways in the troughs and we were violently rocking from side to side. Anything we hadn't stowed—deeply stowed—was sliding across the deck or flying around the cabin. We were hanging on for dear life.

Jamie made his way to the helm, using every handhold available. He turned the key and both engines roared to life. Before gunning us forward, however, he kept the throttles on low and placed us in reverse. A moment later, shreds of rope floated to the surface.

"Right on," said Jamie, who left the cabin to look at the debris. "I was hoping that would happen. The line wrapped around the shaft, but it didn't get all jammed. I was afraid we'd have to send ole' David down with a snorkel. This is great."

Jamie returned to the helm, and a moment later he had us out of the troughs and was easily taking waves on the front quarter. This made for a much smoother ride. He picked up the VHF.

"Vagabond. Just for the Halibut."

"Just for the Halibut. Vagabond. How's it going, Jamie?" came the reply.

"We're free of the line and are on our way. The engines are working well. We're heading back to the marina now."

"Great news! I've been sittin' here wondering, but Dan hooked into a monster and is working on landing the sucker now," said Rick.

"Okay, go give him a hand. Thanks for the help," said Jamie.

"Wasn't nuthin'. See you back at the ranch," said Rick.

"Yeah, see you later. Just for the Halibut returning to channel one-six. Out," said Jamie.

"Vagabond out," said Rick.

"Hey! Does someone have a towel?" asked David.

Later, after all the fish, all the adventure, and all the beauty, I sat in the window seat of the airplane, just after takeoff on our flight back to Minnesota. I looked down at the enormous peaks and the lakes and rivers and all the rugged beauty that is Alaska and had two questions: *What took me so long to get here?* And, *when can I go back?*

● ● ● ●

Two years after I told Ginny my idea for a new business, it became a reality. I stepped off the beaten path of employment, and onto the sidetrack of entrepreneurialism. I had my friend, Larry, arrange some banking, rented a building in Minneapolis, built a couple of laser systems, hired a couple of technical people, and in 1990, Spectralytics was born.

My son, Troy, was our first production worker. It was a job-shop that developed processes for customers' specific components. For example, our first process was to laser-weld absolute pressure sensors used in airplane engines in a vacuum vessel. After that, we did all kinds of laser-cutting jobs: cut sheet metal, wooden ornaments, you name it. Anything to pay rent and make payroll.

In 1991, I went to a medical trade show. The medical device industry seemed like the perfect fit for what we were doing. Happily, the medical industry thought so, too. It wasn't long before all our business came from that sector. In 1998, Spectralytics bought a 21,000-square-foot building in Dassel, Minnesota. We were well on our way.

Those were busy years. They were years of working long days, building clientele and capacity. Ginny was a terrific support. I could not have asked for a better mate.

● ● ● ●

A "little" Alaskan halibut.

30 • ELK DUO, UH . . . ?

IN THE LATE '90'S, MY friend, Brandon, drove with me on a 17-hour ride to Sawtooth Mountain, near Craig, Colorado. It's a grueling drive, but worth it. The hunting is usually excellent, and the beauty of the place is stunning. Northern Minnesota and Southwestern Ontario are both beautiful parts of the world, but Colorado has its own kind of beauty. There is a different feel to the place, and I enjoyed the change. Slow rivers serpentine through wide valleys. Low hills give rise to sharp-edged mountain peaks that challenge a deep blue sky. Groves of aspen trees glow golden in low autumn light, cast long shadows in the winter, and cover the mountains in blankets of green in spring and summer. The words that formed in my mind when I first saw this area was, "God's country." There are a lot of different kinds of churches in the world, and this is one of them.

That year, Brandon and I arrived late in the fall. Snow was already on the ground. We made camp, turned in early, and rose early the next morning. After breakfast, we planned to hunt separately and meet up later in the day. Brandon went left, and I went right.

I was sneak-hunting up a nice snow-covered aspen slope and got within about 900 feet of the treeline when I spotted something buff colored. I put my rifle scope on it. Sure enough, I could see a patch of horn. It was a good-sized bull elk. I didn't have a clear shot at it, though. I would have to shoot between two aspen trees about a foot apart, but that wasn't as much the problem as the position of the elk: it was facing away from me. I stood silently for several moments before he turned sideways. I had a shot to the vitals and I took it. After blinking away the shot, I looked through the scope for the bull, but it was like he vanished. I missed!

Just then, I saw what I thought was the same bull a little farther up the hill. I pulled down on him. In the moment I took the shot, I felt certain that I'd missed this time too, so I was relieved to see the big elk drop in his tracks. Then I spotted another bull bolt up the hill. That must have been the first one that I'd missed.

I trudged through the snow, up the slope to where the elk was. It had been a clean, quick kill. I decided to have a look around the area, particularly to where I'd seen it the first time. To my utter shock, I found a second dead elk! Apparently, I hadn't missed that first shot. There had been three elk there. I actually did kill the first one, but when I saw the second one close by on the other side of the tree, I thought it was the same one, still alive.

I hadn't meant to kill two of them—especially since I could only take one, per the limitation of my tag. I gutted both animals and went to find Brandon. It was easy enough to track him in the snow, the hard part came when I tried to explain to him what happened.

"Ah . . . er . . . well . . . it's like this . . ." It took a while for me to get it out.

Brandon listened and summarized, "You shot two bull elks, but you only have a tag for one, so now you want me to put my tag on your kill."

"Ah . . ." I felt so bad. "Yeah."

He wasn't happy about the idea, but he reluctantly agreed. The hunt was over.

It's good to have friends. Together we returned to the two carcasses. That was a lot of meat to pack out. We loaded up as much as we could and made the first trip over two miles, through snow, to a forest service road where we would later load up our vehicle.

"You couldn't have shot 'em closer to a road?" grumbled Brandon as he staggered under the weight of his pack.

The hunter and horse who helped Brandon and me haul our two elk to the road.

On the way back for our second load, we happened across another hunter on horseback.

"Hello!" he called.

"Hi there! You looking for elk?" I asked, nodding at his rifle.

"Sure am. How about you?"

"Actually, I—we just shot a couple up the hill. We're packing the meat out now," I said.

"Two of them you say?"

"Yeah. There was a third one with them. He might still be around." Eyeing his horse, I tentatively asked, "Hey, you wouldn't by any chance want to make a few bucks and give us a hand packing the meat out?"

The man thought about it for a moment while he reached down to stroke the Black mare's neck. It was almost like he was conferring with her about it. He sat back up and said, "I suppose we could do that."

"Right on," I said.

"Praise Jesus," muttered Brandon. I couldn't blame him. For $100, the man and his horse carried the rest of the meat to the place by the service road. He saved us who-knew how many trips, burdened under heavy loads.

It's good to know that when I miss-count elk, I can still count on people.

● ● ● ●

31 • CHARACTERS: TWO LEGGED AND FOUR

AFTER GETTING SO LUCKY BY meeting that guy who hauled our meat out on horseback, Brandon and I decided to hire some horses the next year when we went back to Meeker. We liked the idea of having a horse do the heavy lifting, and we also wanted to get deeper into the Flat Tops backcountry, away from the main campground. It was getting into late autumn, but it was unseasonably warm and dry, which didn't hurt my feelings at all.

We used a pack outfit called Lone Tom Outfitting. They specialized in hunting mountain lions. Sometimes a mountain lion is referred to as a cougar, or sometimes as a "lone Tom," hence the name of the outfitter. We drove to a trailhead, where we met the guide who would bring us the rest of the way up the mountain to a distant camp.

Our guide—let's just call him Tom—was quite a character. He was a diamond in the rough, emphasis on rough. He was tall and lanky and sported a mountain-man's beard. He had watery blue eyes that hardly ever settled on one thing. His hands were a filthy greenish-brown color; it looked like he'd been playing marbles with horse turds.

Tom stuck his hand out to me and said, "Tom's the name. Pleased to meetcha."

I shook his rough hand, "Gary. This is Brandon."

When Tom and Brandon shook, I could tell Brandon was

probably thinking something like, *Does this guy use toilet paper?* I know this because I wondered it myself.

"So, you guys gettin' away from the missus for some mountain time?" he asked as he pulled a pouch of rolling tobacco from inside his quilted vest.

"I don't know about that," I said, watching him roll a cigarette. "It's not so much about getting away as it is about going to."

Tom nodded sagely, "You know Gary, that's a good philosophy. Not gettin' away, but goin' to. I like that."

Brandon asked, "Are you married?"

Tom said, "Yup."

"Do you have kids?"

"Naw. Lucked out. The missus was spayed before I met her." Tom lit up his rolley and Brandon and I laughed. Despite his rough ways and dirty hands, he had a good sense of humor. I liked him.

The plan was for the three of us to ride horseback up the mountain to the higher camp. He would leave us and then come back to check on us in a few days. He would bring a pack horse with him in case we needed it to bring meat back down the mountain. In a week, Brandon and I would return to the trail head with the three horses.

We made our way up the mountain to a camping spot. Tom took the lead, Brandon followed him, and I brought up the end.

As we moved through the Colorado hills, making our way steadily upward to an eventual elevation of about 8,000 feet, my mind wandered back to when I was a kid on the farm. I had a horse named Baldy. He was a foul-tempered, devious animal. He bucked me off, rubbed me against fences, took off on mad gallops while I was on board, stopped suddenly so I flew over his head, and even bit me. I learned how to ride horses, but they've never been my transportation of choice, and I would never call myself an equestrian. Putting that aside in the moment, however, it was a very pleasant ride through the forest, overlooking a valley thick with trees. We had just entered a clear spot where the sun could reach the ground, when my stomach growled.

"Hey, Tom, let's stop here for a minute. I need to stretch my legs," I said.

"Yup," said Tom. He gently pulled back on the reins and his horse stopped, then dropped its head to find grass.

I slid out of the saddle and walked off the sensation of being bowlegged. Then I rummaged through one of the packhorse's panniers until I found what I was looking for. There was a big bag of beef jerky that I'd been craving. I found a log to sit on and then opened the bag. Brandon came to join me. We sat chewing companionably as we watched Tom check the horses. He cinched straps and checked buckles, inspected hooves, and readjusted saddle blankets. Then he strolled over to where Brandon and I were sitting.

"Want some?" I asked, holding the bag of jerky out to him.

"Thank you kindly," he reached out with his green, tobacco-stained, horse-turd fingers and snatched up a big slab of it. He folded it in half and stuffed it into his shirt pocket. Then he grabbed a second piece and started gnawing on it like a dog on a bone! Brandon and I cracked up.

We got to camp in the early afternoon. He shared a quick meal with us. He mounted his horse and pointed it back down the trail. Just before he disappeared into the trees, he turned in the saddle and said, "Enjoy yourselves. See ya soon.

The next morning, Brandon and I hunted by foot. We walked quickly in the coming daylight until we started to see signs of elk, then we slowed right down for some spotting and stalking.

We didn't have any luck that first day, so the next day we split up. Still, no luck.

In fact, we had no luck for the rest of the week. Our provisions were practically gone, and it was time to give it up. All we had to show for our week in the wilderness was a lot of facial hair. I had a nasty blister on one toe, and Brandon had a sore back.

We saddled up two horses and loaded panniers onto the third. I was riding a stallion American quarter horse, and Brandon had a standardbred mare. The packhorse mare that Tom had dropped off for us was a sturdy Rocky Mountain horse named June. Since Brandon had the sore back, I took charge of June.

My stallion, Ash, was mild-mannered. He giddyuped when I said, "Giddyup," and whoaed when I said, "Whoa." He never acted up and had a lot of patience. Brandon's mare, however, was a horse of a different color. Her name was Lady, but that might have been a misnomer. We were on the trail for no more than 10 minutes when she bucked him off, leaving him sprawling on the ground, gasping for air like a landed trout. Lady trotted merrily down the trail, sans rider.

"You okay?" I asked from the saddle.

"Hhhh . . . Hhhh . . . Hhhh . . ." wheezed Brandon.

I took that to mean, "I'm fine, thank you for asking," so I untied the packhorse and dropped her tether next to Brandon, and headed off to collect Lady. When I found her, she was nibbling grass in an open meadow, happy as could be. She paid me no mind until I reached down from my saddle and took up her reins. She did not want to leave that nice grassy patch.

"I don't care what you want, you're coming with me, Lady," I told her.

She looked at me with big, innocent eyes.

"Don't you look at me like that. I know what you're all about. Can't fool me twice," I said.

She tossed her head like a petulant high-school cheerleader as I led her back to her stranded rider. When we returned, Brandon had recovered his breath and was back on his feet.

"You want to try that again?" I asked, handing him Lady's reins.

"Sure, but without the bucking part," Brandon took the reins and was checking the saddle as I retrieved June. "Oh—" said Brandon.

"What?" I asked.

"There's a strap missing from the saddle," he replied. "There's no way I'm going to be able to keep it from moving around."

"Is it rideable?" I asked.

"I think so, but I'll have to be careful." I watched as Brandon cautiously placed his foot in a stirrup, a hand on the saddle horn, and pulled himself up into position.

"It seems to be holding," I said.

Brandon wiggled around and declared it sturdy enough, so we set off down the trail again. I followed Brandon and led June. June did not seem very appreciative of her lot in life. Leading her was like towing a rudderless boat. She kept zigzagging across the trail from one tree to the next, rubbing against them to rid herself of the panniers. I had to keep tugging on her tether and goading her along. "Come on June! Are you a horse or a mule?"

Meanwhile, ahead of me, Lady kept detouring into every grassy patch she saw. I think in her language, "Whoa" must have meant "Let's stop for grass," and "Giddyup" must have meant "Let's stop for grass."

At one particularly steep part of the trail, Brandon shouted, "HEY!" I looked over just in time to see the saddle slowly slide over Lady's withers, down her neck, and stop just short of her ears. The poor mare's nose was touching the ground with the weight of saddle and rider up around her head. Brandon jumped off and adjusted the saddle. Lady glared at him. June rubbed against a tree. This was getting to be quite the circus.

Brandon led Lady past the steep area and then re-mounted. Aside from constantly tugging June along, and the contest of wills between Brandon and Lady (I'd say it was about a 60/40 lead for Brandon), we managed to make our way down the mountain without any more incidents. When we were about half-way down, the trail led us to a clearing, where we saw a couple of horses drinking from a stream, and two older guys sitting nearby eating trail mix.

Lady decided to join them and began trotting down the trail with Brandon bouncing up and down, tugging on her reins saying, "Whoa! Whoa!" the whole way. The saddle started to shift forward again, and by the time horse and rider arrived at the stream, Brandon was again sitting on Lady's neck, clutching her ears.

The two old guys were cackling at Brandon and Lady like those two old-guy Muppets who sat in the box-seat and heckled everyone. Brandon removed the defective saddle from the wayward horse and let her drink and make friends with the other horses. Meanwhile, I dismounted Ash and let him and June drink as well.

We introduced ourselves to the two older guys, Sam and Hugh.

"We've been hunting around here for, what?" Sam looked at Hugh.

"'Bout 40 years, I guess," answered Hugh.

"Bad year, though," said Sam.

"Bad year," said Hugh, shaking his head.

"Why is that?" asked Brandon.

"It's too hot!" said Sam, agitated.

"Too hot!" agreed Hugh, nodding. "Can't find the elk when it's hot like this."

"Should be snowing by now," said Sam.

"Should be snowing," agreed Hugh, nodding some more. He reminded me of a bobble-head.

"One year," said Sam, "it'd been hot like this, but then over-night a cold front rolled in and brought snow with it. Hugh and I were watching a hill across a valley, and we could see hundreds of elk walking down the mountain."

"Hundreds!" said Hugh, shaking his head in wonder.

"It's like a big, brown waterfall was pouring down the mountain before that snow," said Sam.

"Yup. A big, brown, elk waterfall," said Hugh, finally still, looking off into the distance as though watching it happen all over again.

"I don't think we'll be seeing snow anytime soon," said Brandon.

"No, I don't think we will," said Sam.

"No, don't think so," said Hugh.

Soon after, Brandon re-saddled Lady and we continued our trip down the trail. As we steadily rode down the mountain, I couldn't help thinking about what the old guys had said. In my mind's eye, I could see a snow-capped mountain, with a thin, gold-leaf aspen forest below the treeline, and a hundred elk pouring down the hill like a big, brown, elk waterfall. That would be something to see.

Yup. That really would be something to see.

● ● ● ●

32 • COYOTES' CRIES

A FEW YEARS LATER I went to the Routt National Forest with my friends Rick and Mike. I unfortunately arrived without a tag. In this area, you enter a lottery for permission to shoot an elk—or "draw a tag." I did not have the luck of the draw, but the draw of the Colorado mountains with their clear, blue skies and shimmering golden aspen leaves was irresistible. I thought I could still make myself useful to Rick and Mike, who did draw tags, by being the guide, camp cook, and pack mule. I would hunt vicariously.

Rick, Mike, and I set up my 12x18 wall tent at about 8,400 feet, and we all enjoyed an early evening in front of the fire, planning our strategy for the following day.

We were up and on the trail by 4:00 a.m. Now, I've always been a bit of an early riser when it comes to fishing and hunting trips, so I had no problem getting up and at it by four o'clock, but the steep hill we had to climb at 8,400 feet was a killer. We rose 500 feet over a mile-and-a-half. I enjoy physicality as much as the next guy, but we were all sucking wind that morning.

We were nearing the top of the hill when we heard a bull elk bugle about 300 yards away.

"Shh!" hissed Rick. "Listen," he whispered.

They repeated the shrill, high-pitched bugling. We called back in loud, squeaky tones, "Eeeee Eeeee!" We hoped we sounded like a cow elk, but I fear we more resembled a loose fan belt.

We didn't want him to approach us, because it was still too dark to legally shoot. However, we didn't want him to go too far away either. Mike and I left Rick at that spot to romance the bull elsewhere until the sky grew lighter.

"Hang tight, and when its light enough to shoot, try to walk in on him," I recommended to Rick.

He replied by saying, "Eeeeee Eeeee!"

Mike and I continued up the hill to a place where I thought the elk might run through if we spooked him. On our way up, we heard Rick fire his Magnum. It was still too soon to be shooting elk, so we decided to turn around and go back to see if he needed help.

As we made our way down the steep hill in the dark, every single hair on my body suddenly stood on end. Mike and I stopped in our tracks. At first, I couldn't logic my way to understanding why my body had stopped and was now breathing hard, frozen-limbed, stomach-churning, and cold-sweating; my sympathetic nervous system had taken over. Then I heard a soft growl that made my bowels rumble.

The growl increased in intensity. Then I heard a second one behind Mike and me. A third came from our nine o'clock, then our three o'clock, then from every point on the clock. Then, the low growls erupted into the high barking of coyotes. There was a cacophony of barking, yipping, and howling—the likes of which I'd never heard before or since.

A pack of howling coyotes is not like a pack of howling wolves. Wolves have a low, almost melodic, haunting pack-howl. Coyotes have a kind of grief-stricken, keening quality. It's like they are screaming, but they aren't screaming like Earth-bound creatures, they're screaming like something out of a post-traumatic nightmare. It's incredibly loud and high-pitched. It's not one long note, but many notes that slide together up and down like the melody a mad organist might pound out before swallowing arsenic. They punctuated the screaming with high barks and yipping; each one a murderous stab. It was The. Creepiest. Sound.

As it began, so it ended. We were surrounded, then we weren't. The spirits had tested us, found us unworthy, and moved along.

Relieved that my bowels hadn't betrayed me, I turned to Mike and said, "L-Let's go." He just nodded and stumbled on, down the hill.

When we got to Rick, we found him sitting where we'd left him, but he was white as a shroud and clearly shaken.

"They were everywhere!" he told us. "First, there were just a couple of them up on that rocky area," he pointed toward a jagged outcropping of bare stone. "They were lookin' at me like I was a Big Mac. I mean, they looked like they were starving and I was their next meal. It was freaky, but I didn't feel like they were any big threat at first. You know what I mean?"

We nodded, but truthfully, after what Mike and I had just experienced, I had a hard time *not* imagining a pack of coyotes as a threat.

Rick continued his story, "So yeah, I can't say I liked the way they were looking at me, but then the one on the rock started yipping, and then howling. The next thing I knew I must've been surrounded by about a dozen coyotes, all howling—but it wasn't howling, it was more like . . . screaming, or . . ." His eyes were huge, and he looked at us imploringly, "Do you know what I mean?"

Mike answered for both of us, "Buddy, trust me, we get it. We just got the same treatment on our way back." He looked to me for confirmation and I solemnly nodded. "That was crazy," he added.

"Spooky crazy," said Rick.

"Creepy crazy," agreed Mike.

"It was like assault and battery with sound," I said.

They both looked at me and nodded, eyes wide, "Exactly."

After a moment, Rick continued, "Anyway, I was pretty freaked out, and they kept coming closer and closer, so I fired at the closest one. They got the message. They stopped howling and moved on."

"Yeah, right toward us," Mike said.

I said. "I'm just glad no one got hurt." *And that I never soiled my drawers.*

Mike and I left Rick a second time and hiked back up the brutal slope. It was just sunrise when we came to an old fence line with a calf elk crossing it, about 100 yards away. Following the calf were a couple of cows, but we let them pass. Then came a spike bull; still too young, not legal; then came a raghorn bull, also too young, barely legal. Following the raghorn came a 5x5 bull. Legal. Very legal. My fingers itched for the trigger of my rifle, but of course, I wasn't carrying a rifle since I wasn't hunting. Mike took the shot, but the bull was moving fast, and he missed. I thought of my dad's lesson about not leading 'em enough and I guessed what went wrong. Then a 6x6 bull came along, bringing up the end of the line, but Mike had already spent a shot and wasn't ready for him. In a moment, the whole herd vanished in the trees.

Just to be sure, we walked the trail where we'd just been shooting, but neither of us could find any kind of blood trail. Mike had simply missed the shot. He wasn't happy.

We tracked the herd for about 500-600 yards when we came upon a meadow. There was a nice cow grazing there about 150 yards away from Mike. He raised his gun, aimed, and dropped her. Now he was happy.

In the meantime, further down the mountain, Rick had continued to make like a cow seducing a bull, however it wasn't the bull who showed up, but a cow! Maybe she was the jealous type. Whatever she was, she was destined for Rick's deep freeze.

It was 8:00 a.m. and we had two elk. That's when the real work began. It took us two days to get the meat off the mountain, but not all of it. Little did we know that there would be a tax to pay. We hung two-thirds of Rick's elk up in a tree before we left that first day. We carried the one third down to camp. The next day, we returned to find that the coyotes had managed to eat half a hind-quarter.

This was the first time in all my years hunting that I'd ever lost meat to a wolf, or a bear, or in this case, a pack of hungry coyotes. I figured the pack decided to settle for second best: if they couldn't eat Rick himself, at least they'd eat his kill. Rick called it lucky, and we got on with the job of moving the rest of the meat down the mountain.

● ● ● ●

33 ● SOCIALLY DEFICIENT CAPTAIN AL

ONE SUMMER, LARRY AND I decided on a fishing trip to Seward, Alaska. Snow-capped mountains, glaciers, and fiords surround it. Although it is a cruise-ship port, that didn't bother Larry or me because we were out on a fishing boat when hordes of tourists took over the town. By the time we returned, the ships were gone, leaving us alone to enjoy the low midnight sun over the sparkling city lights.

Our goal was to slay halibut. I'd had so much fun fishing for "hali" last time I was in Alaska that I got hooked on it—so to speak. We booked ourselves on a fishing charter boat. It was a six-pack, meaning there was room for six people to fish, plus a skipper. The skipper was a guy named Al; that was about all we knew about him at the time.

We didn't know who the other four people would be until we arrived at the boat. There was one couple already on board when we got there: Jake and Sally, newlyweds from Rochester, New York. After we introduced ourselves, I asked, "Have you seen our skipper around yet?"

Jake and Sally exchanged a look, then Jake said, "We've met him all right. We asked around about who the best fishing guide in town was and everyone said Captain Al, but everyone also had something to add about his personality. Now that we've met him, I can see why."

"Why?" asked Larry.

Jake said, "He's a little . . . he's somewhat . . . well, he's sort of . . ."

"Socially deficient," said Sally firmly. "The man is socially deficient."

Larry and I thought about that for a moment. "Okay," I said, "I'm good with that as long as the man can find me some halibut."

"Yup. I agree," said Larry.

Sally looked dubious but said, "Of course, I mean that's his main function here. That's what matters the most." As it would turn out, social skills do matter in a fishing captain. I might have recalled this fact from our encounter with Captain Diehard, but at the time all I was thinking about was halibut.

Soon, two more guys came down the ramp and along the dock to the boat. They introduced themselves as Nick and Cam, chartered accountants in the great state of Texas for most of the year, and sport halibut hunters in Alaska in the summertime. Then came Captain Al.

He looked like a guy from a police lineup.

I don't know that I've ever seen a filthier man. He was literally slick with slime. His overalls were covered in fish blood (at least I hoped it was from fish) and shone with slime. He had a beard that made him look like a wilder and crazier Abe Lincoln. His hair was matted under a brown ball cap, or at least it was brown by the time I got to see it. His hands were black with grime. When he opened his mouth to speak, he revealed decades of plaque and tooth decay.

"I'm Captain Al. It's going to take us two hours to get to the reef where we're gonna fish. You gotta sit in the cabin on the way out. Let's go." Yup, the guy had the personality of a gaff hook.

I was willing to overlook the personality issue, but I was seriously unimpressed when I first stepped into the cabin. *Was this guy raised by vultures?* I thought the man himself was filthy, but the cabin of his boat was disgusting. The stench was like getting slapped in the face with a rotten salmon. Take decaying fish, mix it with a football team's locker room, throw in some black mold, and you've got what the cabin of the boat smelled like. I made a beeline straight for the seat next to the open window. You'd think that living on a dairy farm for the first 18 years of my life would have conditioned me to bad smells, but you'd think wrong. I was like a dog in a moving car for the next two hours: my nose stuck six inches out the window, panting for air.

Two hours later, Al pulled back the throttles and we slowed to a stop. The six of us anglers stampeded for the door and gulped in the clean, clear, fresh air on the back deck. We were all very relieved to get out of that awful cabin.

As Al went about setting the anchor in 100 feet of water, Sally pulled out her lunchbox and pulled out a banana. She peeled it and was about to take a bite when suddenly Al yelled at her, "HEY!"

She startled and snapped her mouth closed.

"You can't eat that banana!" cried Al.

Sally looked at the fruit in confusion, "Why not?"

"It's bad luck to have bananas on a boat! Don't you know that?" Then, Al grabbed the banana out of her hand and threw it overboard.

"Hey!" Sally protested.

Then, Al saw that there was another banana in her lunchbox, so he stuck his grubby hand into the box, grabbed the banana, shook it in her face while making a kind of growling noise, and threw that one overboard too.

Jake said, "What the—hey! Stop that!"

That only caught Al's attention. Undeterred, Al said, "How

'bout you? You got bananas in your lunchbox too?" He snatched the silver box from under Jake's bench and opened it. "AHA!" he crowed. He took two more bananas out and chucked them into the ocean.

The rest of us watched the bizarre events with amused disbelief. We all hid our half-smiles and shook our heads in wonder. I know I was thinking how glad I was that I hadn't brought any bananas with me. If anyone else brought some, they weren't letting on. Jake and Sally were not impressed. Al didn't care.

My fishing began when I lowered some herring on a hook with a two-ounce ball and bounced it off the bottom, about 110 feet down. *Fishy fishy in the brook, please come and bite my hook.* My aunt Eldora's tune popped into my head, and it worked! I soon had a strike that felt like the bottom of the ocean, except that the bottom moved. It took nearly 10 minutes to get the halibut up. It came up slow and steady, then as soon as it hit the surface, it started thrashing. We could see that it was a fair size. When it spooked, I let it have some line. Once it calmed down again, I reeled some more. I brought it in closer to the boat and Al stood next to me with a gaff hook ready. He expertly drove the harpoon into the fish where it would do maximum damage. It took two guys to pull it over the gunwale, then all 85 pounds of it flopped onto the deck. A halibut can do a lot of damage if you don't kill it, or at least bleed it well, before landing it. Al did a fine job. He had it killed, the hooks out, and on ice before you could say "Fish on."

"Nice hali!" said Larry.

"Thanks!" I said, proudly.

Next, one of the other guys, Cam, caught a "chicken," or a small halibut. This one didn't need the gaff, and Al was busy baiting hooks, so I grabbed the net to help Cam land his chicken. I nearly jumped out of my skin when someone grabbed my arm from behind and shouted, "HEY!" into my ear.

"DON'T TOUCH MY NET!" shouted Al.

"OK!" I passed the net off to him like a hot potato. The guy was nearly foaming at the mouth. Al took over from me and scooped the chicken from the sea as I watched, wondering if he might be so deranged that he was dangerous. *Naw . . .*

I dropped another line. We really were in a good spot because it was only down for a couple of minutes before my rod bent like a preacher's head saying grace before a nice fish dinner. This one was significantly bigger than the last one, I could tell. I was working hard reeling it in; my arm burned from cranking and cranking.

"I got one too!" I heard Nick call, excitedly. "Holy! This thing's huge!" He and I both reeled hard. We were both pulling in monsters!

"Whoa!" I said excitedly, "This one's huge too!"

"He's really fighting me!" said Nick.

"Yeah! This one's a fighter too!" I said.

We reeled and reeled and reeled. Then, Al leaned over my side of the boat, then crossed to Nick's side of the boat and grunted. Then, he came back to my side, opened a knife, and cut my line!

"What'd you do that for?" I demanded.

"You're both hooked on the same fish," he said.

I was thunderstruck. "So, what, you cut *my* line? I've been on it for 10 minutes! I had it first." Was he punishing me because I grabbed that net earlier?

Just then, the monster broke the surface with wild thrashing and everyone's attention was on the fish instead of my outrage—even my own attention shifted to the fish.

"Give him line! Give him line!" I shouted when the hali dove again, but Nick kept trying to hold on. Then, he let the line run for a while.

Cam said, "Okay, now bring him back."

"Easy, easy," said Sally.

"Get him closer to the boat," said Jake.

There's never a shortage of advice on a fishing charter.

Captain Al neatly harpooned it, and he and Cam pulled it aboard. We later weighed it at 125 pounds. It should have been mine.

Larry, in the meantime, had caught nothing. He was frustrated. Everyone around him was landing big fish, and he hadn't even had a nibble.

"You didn't bring any bananas, did you?" I quietly asked him. He snorted.

Just then, I got another strike. I was on fire! I pulled this one up, and Captain Al helped me land it. It was slightly smaller than my first, but still a very respectable fish. My adrenaline was up, and I was very happy. That was my limit for halibut, so Al swapped my pool-cue-sized halibut rod for a smaller one, and I started fishing for silver salmon, or coho, as some people call them. It wasn't long before I limited out on those too. I was over-the-moon happy!

Having caught my limits, I put my rod away and poured a cup of tea from the thermos. I took a back seat on the deck and watched the others fish. It turned out to be a good show. The bite was on! All of a sudden, it was like everyone had a fish on their line and was working their rod. Captain Al was busier than a one-eyed cat watching five mouse holes. Having been chewed out for touching Al's gear once before, I knew better than to offer help. Jake, however, did not.

Sally hooked a good-sized halibut and was struggling to bring it up. I could tell she was tiring. The pace of her reeling had become slow, and the tip of the rod got closer and closer to the water. Just when it looked like she might lose the whole shebang, her husband slipped in beside her and helped her raise the tip again.

Captain Al nearly lost his mind when he saw that. "STOP!" he screamed.

Jake jumped, just as I had done when Al screamed at me earlier, only Jake looked angry.

Al said, "Get your hands off that! That's NOT your rod!"

"What—" said Jake.

"Get off get off get off!" said Al. He truly had become our guide to the Twilight Zone.

Jake let go of the rod, but yelled, "What the hell's your problem?"

"My problem? My problem? YOU are my problem! I can lose my license if you even touch her rod!" shouted Al.

"What are you talking about?" shouted Jake. "She was about to lose it overboard!"

"Then let her! Or tell me! You don't touch another angler's rod! DON'T TOUCH!"

"I'll touch whatever I want!"

"Not on MY boat!"

Jake stormed over and got within inches of Captain Al's face. For several moments, the two stood eyeball-to-eyeball, snorting like a couple of bull elk in rutting season.

Then, the halibut Sally had been slowly but steadily reeling in surfaced with a splash, breaking the tension. "*Someone* grab the damn gaff!" she cried.

Jake turned away from Al, and Al grabbed the gaff. He gaffed the fish and pulled it in. It was a nice fish, and I guess it was enough for Jake and Sally because once it was on ice, the couple retreated into the cabin and didn't come out or speak to anyone for the rest of the trip. They must have been incredibly steamed if they were willing to sit in that stinking cabin for hours and forgo any more fishing. I'm not sure who they were trying to punish: themselves or Al.

The rest of the crew limited out on everything, even Larry, who landed two considerably sizeable halibut in addition to his silver salmon. It was one of the best fishing days of my life! For that reason, I gave Captain Al a nice tip, but it sure wasn't for his social skills.

The next year, we returned to the area and I asked about him. They told me that Captain Al had gone commercial fishing. "Charter fishing wasn't really his thing," they said. *You think?* I wondered if our group might have contributed to his decision to stop working with the public. Regardless, I thought it was a smart move on his part.

Note to Al: it's best to play to your strengths and know when to make a move.

● ● ● ●

34 • THE UNIQUENESS OF WATER

FOR ALMOST FOUR DECADES, I've usually been the first guy to go ice fishing on Manuella Lake in the fall. It's a smallish lake near where I live in Minnesota. I test the thickness of the ice with a large ice chisel. If I can thrust it through clear ice in one blow, I'll step back and wait another day. The moment the ice gets to be about three inches thick, I'll tow my ice shack out with my Polaris four-wheeler ATV. Usually, I'm fishing for walleye by December first, but there were a couple years where I was on the ice for Thanksgiving. On the other hand, I've also seen open water at Christmastime.

A fish house is usually a quiet, relaxing place, where I can settle in and let my thoughts wander. For instance, if you think about it, it's pretty wonderful that ice floats. Ice, a solid, floats on water, a fluid. If this weren't the case, water—which covers 75 percent of the planet—would freeze from the bottom up.

Water is unique among all liquids in that it reaches its maximum density at 39°F but doesn't actually freeze until it reaches 32°F. Sometimes, in the fall you will hear people say a lake is "turning over." This is when the layer of water on the surface is denser (39°F) than the water below and then sinks. This continues until the surface water can freeze at 32°F and form the ice that we all know and love for ice fishing!

Occasionally, something other than a fish tugging on my line will interrupt my musings. I've had a muskrat poke his whiskered face out of the spearing hole. One moment I'm alone with my thoughts, the next moment, I'm sharing the shack with a wet rodent looking for a place to warm up. That'll make you jump. A sharp CRACK in the ice under your feet will scare the bejesus out of you, too. It'll have you off your seat and through the door—Looney Tunes style.

The goal is to catch fish and not fall through the ice. Timing is critical. You want to be out there as early as possible because walleye taste particularly delicious at that moment, but you don't want to go too early because you risk falling through the ice and becoming a meal for the walleye.

One year, I might have pushed the season a little too much. I tested the thickness of the ice with my trusty ice chisel, and there were three inches of clear ice where I intended to put the ice house, so I pulled the house out to the spot with my Polaris ATV. All was well. As predicted, the walleye cooperated nicely as I fished all day. By nightfall, I had my limit in a bucket filled with tastiness. I put the bucket on the Polaris and headed back to shore in the dark.

In the moonless night, I had to use the headlights to follow my earlier tracks off the lake. I didn't think there would be any problem getting to shore, but I've been wrong like that before.

CRACK!

I felt the front tires drop, and I immediately bailed off the ATV and assumed the spread-eagle position, distributing my weight over as much ice as I could. A moment later I looked back, and all there was to see was my lonely bucket of fish, bobbing in the water where my Polaris should have been.

I may have lost my ATV, but I'd be darned if I was going to lose my fish too. (Did I mention how good the first ice-caught walleyes of the season taste?) I inched my way on my belly toward the hole and managed to hook onto the rim of the bucket with my fingertips. Carefully, I drew the bucket toward me and gently lifted it onto the ice. Then, I pushed it along the ice ahead of me as I alligator-crawled a safe distance from the hole, and then tippy toed to shore.

I stood up in my water-filled Sorels and looked back to see the Polaris's headlights on, under the ice. Die Hard makes a really good battery.

Two days later, the ice thickened enough for me to retrieve my vehicle. I grabbed my three-ton come-a-long, a 12-foot two-by-four, my chainsaw, and headed for the lake. It was still very early, just barely dawn; I wanted some privacy. The last thing I was in the mood for was to be the source of entertainment for lake-dwellers. That, or I could imagine someone calling 9-1-1. I chose to manage the job alone because, frankly, I was just too embarrassed to ask for help.

I cut two holes about a foot apart, about 10 feet from where the Polaris went through the ice. Then, I threaded a rope down one hole and up the other and tied the two ends together to create a loop, then I attached the winch to it. Using the chainsaw, I cut around the area where the Polaris had fallen through. I used the ice chisel to remove the freed chunks of ice. Next, I shoved the two-by-four into the hole and then under the rear of the Polaris and then slid down a big line with a heavy hook, like I was fishing for ATVs and got lucky. I managed to hook onto the rear frame, or at least something solid. So far so good. Using the winch, I pulled it up to the surface of the water.

Getting the Polaris to the surface of the water wasn't too hard, but getting the ATV onto the ice was tricky. I had to pry the rear wheels above the edge of the ice using the ice chisel. This was no mean feat, but once I had that accomplished, the rest went smoothly. Altogether, it took about one and a half hours to land that fish and get it back on the preferred side of the ice.

I had to push it to shore and winch it onto my trailer to

get it back to my carport. There, I drained all its fluids and emptied the crankcase of water, topped all the fluids back up, and—to my amazed delight—it started on the first pull!

The things I'll do for a fish. The upside of this story is that all the busted ice created a panic among the other local fishermen to the point that I had my honey-hole all to myself for three or four weeks. The walleyes were delicious!

● ● ● ●

35 ● DEAD MEN DON'T TALK

SOMETIMES, IN THE SUMMER, I like to get out by myself and go night fishing on Manuella. It's a wholly different experience from chartering with a group, and I find it entirely relaxing. Every now and then, I launch the boat as the sun goes down and head out on my own, in search of walleyes. There's a 23-foot-deep rock pile near the east center of the lake where I like to slip-bobber fish with leeches for bait.

One warm summer night, I cast my line out into the shiny black water and settled peacefully into the rhythm of fishing. It was a dark night, with only about a quarter-moon, and clouds slipped by at regular intervals.

At some point, my mind hooked onto the recent memory of a piece of local news. A couple of weeks earlier, a man had drowned in this very lake, but no one had yet recovered the body. Only a week ago, they'd held a memorial on the lake, not far from where I was now fishing. There had been a priest and everything. I supposed that explained why I was the only person on the lake that night: everyone else was spooked away. I wasn't spooked away, though. Why wasn't I spooked, too? Good question. Maybe I should have been spooked. Maybe this dark night wasn't so much peaceful as it was spooky... Maybe I should be more concerned about lost bodies in my local fishing hole... *Am I going to find a dead body floating in the night?* Just as my pondering, wandering mind was getting the better of me, I peered down into the black water and *saw a man's pale white face in the water staring up at me with dead eyes!*

I jumped in my seat, sending large ripples out around the boat. I sucked in air and gaped at the bodiless head in the water calmly staring back at me with empty eyes. My jaw worked soundlessly, like a landed fish in its final death throes. I would have screamed, but my voice did not work.

Then the head said, "How's the fishin'?"

All I got out was, "*ee.*"

"Catch anything?" it said, grinning like a jack-o-lantern.

My brain was reeling. The disembodied head of a dead man was asking me about the fishing in the middle of a lake in the middle of the night. Slowly, like in a dream, I started to notice things. First, I saw that in fact, the head wasn't disembodied. It just looked that way in the night. In fact, he had a body and it was treading water; I could just make out the arms waving back and forth. Then, I noticed that his eyes weren't dead at all, they were actually quite lively. And, the guy wasn't grinning, he was just smiling politely. Conclusion: this is not a dead body. I'm smart like that.

Outwardly calm, I replied, "Hu- Pretty good. Got a c-couple walleyes in the live-well."

"Hey! That's great!" said the man-not-disembodied-head.

"What are you doing in the middle of the lake?" I asked.

"I like to swim at night. I swim all the way across and back again. I live on the shore back there," he nodded his head toward the shore behind him.

"Is that such a good idea? Swimming in the dark like that?" I asked. "Aren't you worried about a guy like me running you over with his boat?"

"Naw. I'm good at diving underwater," he said.

I nodded, then said, "You worried about finding a dead body?"

The man shook his head and said, "Probably no more than you are."

"Uh huh," I said, not letting on that I'd been plenty spooked. "Well, I guess it's a nice enough night."

"Sure is. You have a good one. Good luck with the fishing," he said.

"Thanks. You take care," I said.

He swam off and I continued to fish. About three-quarters of an hour later the fish quit biting and I was thinking about calling it a night, when a voice broke the silence from a few feet away.

"Fishin' still good?" asked the swimmer.

I half jumped out of my skin again. *Good grief! Is there nowhere a man can be alone?* "Naw, they stopped biting."

"Too bad," he said. Then, "Well, have a good night," and he carried on swimming toward his home.

"You too."

Note to self: sometimes the scariest place of all is your own imagination.

● ● ● ●

36 ● ALASKA AND BEYOND

IT WAS WITH GREAT ANTICIPATION that I caught a plane from Minnesota to Anchorage, Alaska. Ever since seeing that magnificent state, I'd wanted to hunt an Alaskan moose, so when I had a chance to make the trip, I packed my bags and my gun and caught the first plane out.

In Anchorage, I tried to report my weapon to security at the Penair desk, but the woman told me, "We don't have security here." They do, but I think its called "profiling." Still, you gotta love a place that doesn't worry about your rifle.

Soon, I boarded a Penair 30-passenger turboprop plane to Cold Bay, 618 miles southwest. By this time, I'd already traveled further west than the Hawaiian Islands and I was in my glory. From Cold Bay, I boarded an even smaller plane to a small island airstrip, where I once again switched planes to a—you guessed it—even smaller plane. It was tiny, but that's what made it possible to land on the mini-runway of my last stop: Bear Lake Lodge. From my cramped quarters aboard the miniscule plane, I spotted a grizzly bear and a small herd of caribou, but I didn't see any moose in any of the rolling green hills below.

Once we landed, I deplaned and gave a mighty stretch the moment my shoes touched ground. I watched as the bush pilot unloaded my baggage and several cases of Bud Light. I guess they don't like to waste space on a plane, and the villager who met us was overjoyed to get the free beer transportation.

I'd signed a contract with Bear Lake Lodge and intended to bring home the biggest moose I could find, along with a lot of fish. The lodge is a large-ish outfit that can accommodate 20 guests at a time. The main lodge is situated next to the eight-mile long, glacier-fed lake, and my cabin was situated about 50 feet from a river that was about 150 feet across. The place was well known for its grizzly and brown bears, as well as for its spectacular salmon and dolly varden trout fishing. I wanted it all.

I wasted little time settling into my one-room cabin. I returned to the lodge and scanned a wall with about 40 rods and reels hanging on it. I grabbed a light spinning rod and reel and was casting for dolly varden in the river just moments later. Well, "casting" implies that I cast more than once, when in fact, I landed a nice, big trout on my very first cast. It was about three pounds, and it didn't come willingly.

For my second cast, I tied into a silver salmon. Now, this fish entered the stream from the salty ocean about 18 miles downstream and worked his way up against recently-melted ice water flowing at about seven miles-per-hour. It was one tough fish. I had a major battle on my hands! It took the lure and ran downstream. I had to run about 300 feet to catch up to him and then played him for at least 15 minutes before I could get him landed. It was worth the effort: what a beautiful fish.

Clearly, a heavier pole and stronger line was in order, so I returned to the lodge and swapped out my light spinner for a saltwater rig and heavier line. With that in the water, I could subdue the salmon in five minutes instead of 15. For 45 minutes, I caught fish after fish after fish. I couldn't believe it. I'd been going flat-out and had to take a break. I laid down for

15 and then, feeling like a kid again, jumped out of bed and headed for the water once more. More fish! I'd never seen fish be so cooperative.

Having fished my fill that first day, I shifted my focus to finding a great big moose. The lodge had a 20-power spotting scope on a tripod with wheels, so I could glass about 20 square miles of moose country right there from the lodge. I had two guides, Leo and Joe. The plan was to hunt from a boat on the lake, but the first day of hunting proved to be too windy. The wind came down the mountains and whipped up whitecaps so big that our 16-foot Lund boat couldn't weather it.

Fortunately, the wind settled down the next day and we were on the water at sun up. We navigated to the glacier end of the lake and looked for a prominent foothill where we could call moose and set up our spotting scope.

It was noon when Joe suddenly sat up and pointed, "There!" he whispered excitedly. Leo and I looked to where he was pointing and spotted a moose about a half-mile away.

"Right on," I whispered back and lifted a cow call to my mouth. "Hhunaaa hhunaaa!" I called in my very best cow-moose voice. Leo and Joe used white pail lids to rustle the bush, and represent the palms of a bull moose moving around in the bush. Then, Leo and Joe took turns with the calling. Within a few minutes, we drew the moose in close enough to see his size.

"What do you think, Gary?" asked Joe.

"I don't know . . . he looks a little small to me," I replied.

"Yeah, I think the rack is probably under 50 inches," said Leo.

"I think I'll pass on this one, guys," I decided.

"Sounds about right," agreed Joe.

My guides and I sat on the hill until about 5:00 that evening, when Joe finally caught sight of another bull in a patch of alder trees. It was impossible to tell for certain from that distance, but we thought it's rack might be in the neighborhood of 60 inches. We packed up our gear and motored the boat over to where we saw the moose, beached it, and walked into the area about 400 yards. Sure enough, the moose appeared about a mile away, on the other side of a deep, swift river.

Joe raised the cow call to his mouth and moaned into it.

"Not bad technique," said Leo, "but your volume is too low, and you don't have the moan quite right. You need to sound desirable."

"Desirable," deadpanned Joe.

"Yeah, you gotta make the bull want to come all this way. I mean, he needs to know he's not just wasting his time, you know what I mean?" said Leo.

"And how would you be more 'desirable' Leo?" asked Joe, with amusement in his voice.

Leo seemed to have missed the merriment and said seriously, "Well, I'd give it a lot more volume and then end it with a little guttural grunt." He was oblivious of Joe's sidelong glance to me. "It's the grunt at the end that really gets him going."

"Show us how it's done, Leo," said Joe.

"All right." Leo put the call to his mouth and moaned passionately and loudly, following up with a little guttural grunt.

Joe and I nodded our approval, "That's sexy Leo," said Joe. "Isn't he sexy, Gary?"

"Oh yeah, he's sexy. Absolutely," I agreed, laughing.

"Desirable," added Joe.

"Oh yes, very desirable," I said.

Leo scowled at the two of us giggling like two boys in grade six sex-ed class. "Oh, grow up," he snapped, which only made us laugh harder. "Watch and learn," he said, and raised the call up to his mouth once more and called loudly; he could have been heard in Cold Bay.

"Good one!" said Joe.

"Yup, good and loud," I agreed.

"Okay," nodded Leo, "now we just sit back for the next 20 minutes or so until our bull shows his face.

We nodded and settled down. I was impatient; 20 minutes to me seemed like an hour.

"It's like waitin' by the phone for your crush to call," said Joe. Leo gave him a dirty look, and Joe smirked.

Finally, after a wait that felt longer than adolescence, we heard rustling in the nearby bush.

"Sh," said Joe—all business now, nodding to the bush.

I raised my .300 Weatherby Magnum rifle and aimed toward the noise. About 300 yards away, a huge moose stepped out of the alders. Sure enough, he was a brute. His rack was beautiful. He walked straight toward us and when he got about 70 yards away I figured we'd romanced him enough. I pulled the trigger and double-lunged him. He dropped but the big bruiser managed to get up. He was facing me, kinda like standing dead, and I didn't want to put a round into his horns or ruin the cape, so I held off.

"SHOOT!" screamed Joe.

"FIRE! What are you waiting for?" screamed Leo.

I could see their point. The animal weighed a ton, was wounded, and faced us with a rack the size of Alaska. Still, although he had his feet, he seemed more dazed and confused than aggressive. So, I walked around him until his neck was broadside to me and fired. The round put him down fast.

After we took a few pictures, the hard work began. By then it was about 6:30 p.m., so although we would be missing a meal, we weren't going to run out of daylight for a couple more

The biggest moose I've shot so far.

hours. The kill site was only about 100 yards from the water, so there wasn't much of a portage. We had just enough time to skin him down and put half the meat in the boat, which is all there was room for.

We would have to leave the other half of the meat there at the site overnight, which wouldn't have been a huge worry if it hadn't been for the well-worn bear trail not 50 feet from the pile of fresh meat. Bears, grizzlies in particular, are known to have exceptional noses for sniffing out food. If a bear decided he wanted my moose, it would have my moose. *Please Jesus, protect my moose from bears.* I sent up a quick prayer and hopped into the boat with my guides and meat.

With a full load of moose and three guys, it was a slow but happy eight miles across the lake back to the lodge. We hung the meat in the meat house and securely locked the doors to prevent bear entry. I'd already heard plenty of stories of bears taking what they want. They'll follow the river, gorging on whatever dead fish it gives up, or catch what live ones they can.

They'll also follow the river all the way to the ocean and feed on dead whales or whatever else they can find.

"One year," said Leo, "a grizzly bear apparently smelled something it liked coming from the kitchen sink outlet. It started digging up the drain pipe all the way to the septic tank. Laurie came out into the back yard the next morning and she said that it looked like a backhoe had been working."

Joe nodded, "Yeah, and you remember the time another grizzly got into the barn?"

"Oh yeah!" said Leo, remembering.

"Yeah," Joe looked at me, eyes bright, "he got into the barn and for some reason, got it in his head to drink a pail of red paint!"

"Paint?" I said, "Why would it drink paint?"

"No one can figure," said Leo. "Maybe he thought it was blood or something."

Joe shook his head, "No, I can't see that. A bear knows what blood smells and tastes like. It must have just liked the flavor."

I nodded. That sounded more plausible, albeit weird.

"So anyway, a year goes by and we get a hunter come back to the lodge, saying that he got a grizzly. 'Good for you!' we say, but he had this strange look on his face. 'What?' we asked him, and you know what he said?" Joe and Leo both looked at me with anticipation.

I shook my head, "No, what?"

"He said that the bear's face was all red!"

With all these stories running through my mind, a small part of me had given in to the notion that I might have lost the other half of my moose to a bear. Don't get me wrong, I still had hope, but I was also steeling myself for the worst. So, the next day, when Leo, Joe, and I beached the boat and found the pile of meat just as we had left it, with the hide laid over it all, we were elated. *Thank you, Jesus.*

We finished quartering the moose and sawed the antlers off. In Alaska, it's state law that you must not leave more than five pounds of meat at a kill site. We sawed the ribs off and left only the spinal column. I remembered Charlie Budd and how he had made use of all the organs and even parts of the animal I wouldn't normally consider useable. Once again, we boarded the boat and made our way back to camp. This time I felt much more at ease, knowing that I would not have to share my 1,300 pound moose with a bear.

I still had a week left of my stay at Bear Lake Lodge, so I spent most of it fishing. I kept at it until I had about 50 pounds in the freezer. We hung the moose meat for three days and then cut it up for transport back to the lower States. I left a quarter for the winter caretaker of the camp. I left Alaska with 10, 50-pound boxes of moose and fish, and the memories of a lifetime.

I've been to Alaska several times now and each time it just gets increasingly beautiful. I was there with my son, Troy, on Labor Day. We chartered a small plane that had skis and wheels, and we landed on a glacier. It was a pristine day—flying among the snow-capped peaks, no wind, no clouds, the sky was the bluest of blues. It was just spectacular.

Troy and I then went to Seward and chartered a boat for two days. The first day out, we had been on the water for two hours when Troy caught one fish, turned green, and chummed for the rest of the day. It was too bad for him, because we caught a lot of really, really big ling cod that trip. Really big. Huge.

The next day as luck would have it for Troy, it was too windy to go on the ocean fishing. I got the charter fee back and went to a local sport shop and rented a couple fishing rods. We went to the Resurrection River and caught nine beautiful silver salmon. Troy was much happier to be fishing with his feet firmly on the ground.

Fishing in Alaska.

I don't imagine I'll ever stop going to Alaska. It's the ultimate place for a guy like me. I've fished and hunted all my life and I've always loved it, but in Alaska, the fishing and hunting is like nowhere else in the world. The rawness and sheer scale of the landscapes, and the fresh wilderness—well, now that I've had a taste of it, I can't get enough.

● ● ● ●

37 • CORNERSTONE GAME FEED

IN 2004, I DECIDED IT was time to sell Spectralytics. I had run the company for 14 years and was pleased with what it became. I sold everything, except for some interest in the intellectual properties, to a company called Preco. However, even though I was no longer the owner, I stayed on as President.

In 2005, Larry and I started something that we couldn't possibly have predicted the outcome of. When I look back on it, I often think of that adage, *be careful what you start*. That said, I also think of it all with fondness, and maybe a touch of pride.

"Hey, Gary," asked Larry one fine spring morning, "how much meat do you have in your freezer?"

"A lot. How 'bout you?" I asked.

"Same," he said. "Probably more than my family and I can eat before I start losing some of it to freezer burn."

I thought about that and nodded, "Yeah, that's probably true for me too. What do you have in mind?"

"Why don't you and I put on a game feed for some of the guys at our church? They're always asking about our hunting trips. I think a lot of them would appreciate it. We could use my office for the venue. There's tons of space there."

"I think that's a great idea!" I said.

So that first year, we had about 40 guys from our church in Litchfield, Minnesota, join us at Larry's office space for a wild game feed of fish, venison, ducks, geese, and elk. A few of the other guys donated some of the contents of their own freezers, too, so we had a great variety. We even put together three bowls of salad—two and a half of which went uneaten. Putting aside the group's dislike of lettuce, everyone considered it a wild success.

Word of its popularity spread. The next year, we had our second annual game feed. This time 70 guys and even a few women showed up. We had volunteers donate game and help with the cooking, cleanup, and all the other tasks involved in feeding a big group. That year, we only put out two bowls of salad. Two bowls came back uneaten. We figured this group of people preferred to eat the animals that ate the salads.

There were only 30 more people the second year than there were the first, but I think those 30 must have liked to talk because the third year we had 200 people show up! We moved the event to our new Cornerstone Church and added more menu items. That year and for those to follow, we had the usual wild game like deer, elk, moose, bear, duck, pheasant, and fish, but we also had such exotic meats as turtle, sandhill crane, beaver, and wild boar! Occasionally we had to get creative in the kitchen. We sorted through all that game and some of it was, well, gamey. For instance, one year a guy brought in some pheasant that had been slightly freezer burned. It wasn't the freshest, to say the least. After cooking them for half a day, Larry held a piece out to me and said, "What on earth am I supposed to do with this?"

It was not going to make for an attractive dish, and we had tons of the stuff. I examined the meat, leaned in toward Larry, and whispered, "Gravy."

That was the secret sauce that year, and every bit of that pheasant disappeared. In fact, since we never served salad again, there were very few leftovers at all.

The sixth year, a couple months before the game feed, Pastor Paul approached Larry and me. "I think we should hold the event over two nights this year."

"T-TWO nights?" I sputtered.

"Sure," said the pastor, "it makes sense. It's become such a popular event that we can't possibly feed everyone who wants to come in just one night."

"Oh, I don't know about that," I said, shaking my head. I was imagining the amount of work that would be involved. I looked to Larry, "What do you think?"

Larry nodded thoughtfully, which surprised me. I assumed he would balk at the idea too. He said, "I can see the pastor's point. It's grown every year, and we must think that it'll be even bigger this year than it was last year. It kind of makes sense to do it over the two nights."

"It's just so much work," I said.

"True," said Pastor Paul, "but we can recruit as many volunteers as we need. We'll put out the word that we need more help, and I trust that people will step up."

I nodded. That was true. Any time we needed help we just had to ask the congregation and help arrived. I had no doubt that the number of people we needed would show up and get the job done. It was one of the things I loved about our church. "I guess we could look at it."

Pastor Paul's face lit up with a smile, "Excellent!"

"So," asked Larry, "what weekend did you have in mind?"

That is how we ended up serving wild game to about 500 hungry souls over two nights. We served about 600 pounds of game and fish, and had more than 60 volunteers working in the kitchen, doing the decorating, and serving. We started thawing things out on Wednesday, cooking on Thursday, and served on Friday and Saturday. Guys brought in all kinds of meats. The two most popular dishes, however, weren't all that exotic:

they were fish (sunnies, crappies, and walleye), and meatloaf of many varieties. I remember seeing one guy walk away with a plate heaping with meatloaf and nothing else.

All these years, we've been running what has come to be known as the Cornerstone Game Feed. The best part of the event, in my opinion, is to see the number of lives changed by the inspirational message of the Word. The response has been huge. The event is powerful and uplifting for everyone. It still is a very gratifying undertaking and something everyone looks forward to every year. It has become the foundation of a vibrant Men's Ministry at Cornerstone. We couldn't possibly have known what we were getting into on that innocent day so many years earlier. And yes, I've learned to be careful what I start.

* * * *

38 • A BLOODY MESS

YOU PRETTY MUCH ALWAYS TAKE a risk when you take a side-track. Sidetracks are about fun and adventure, but they're also filled with risk. Risks being what they are, eventually something is not going to go your way. Sometimes, when you take a sidetrack, you end up in a bloody mess.

Of my many snowmobile trips in Montana, Wyoming, South Dakota, Minnesota, Wisconsin, and Michigan, the most memorable for me, by far, was the one to Cooke City, Montana. A bunch of us guys were staying at the Skyline Guest Ranch, about four miles from Cooke City.

It was a beautiful, clear, crisp day and we were all anxious to make the first run up the nearby mountains. We unloaded the snowmobiles from our trailers and rode them on an unplowed highway about 10 miles to the ranch. That's where we started our adventure.

There's an average of about 400 inches of snowfall there every year, so it's fair to say we had a good base to sled on. We had a great morning of mountain climbing with our machines. The snow was well-packed, and the sky was brilliant blue. By about one o'clock, we were all getting hungry. Breakfast seemed like a long time past. I could already taste lunch at the Prospector Restaurant in Cooke City. Still, I was having a great time on the snowmobile, so I decided to make one last run up the mountain. With the packed snow, I could climb as high as I wanted, and I did. When I eventually pointed the sled back down the hill, I realized that I didn't quite have the braking ability that I needed. The packing of the snow that made it such a joy to climb the mountain was the same thing that made it hard to slow down on the flipside. Oops!

The snowmobile was still new to me, so I made a second misjudgment. I was fast gaining speed and suddenly there was a snow drift, about four feet high, right in front of me. *No problem, I'll just jump it,* I thought. However, I didn't count on the sled with its rider-forward design being a bit nose-heavy. I hit the drift and launched skyward, but the nose pointed nearly straight down, and I had no time to get it leveled off before landing. I smashed into the hard-pack nose-first. I bailed off to the side but in that process, a piece of the sled bit me hard.

There I lay, gasping and stunned. My snowmobile somehow landed upright, stalled, and coasted on down the mountain without me. In utter disbelief, I watched it scoot down the hill, sans rider. At that moment, I had some serious abandonment issues. The air around me was crisp and cold and silent, save for the *whrrr* of the sled's track rolling over the snow. The sled found the edge of a large crater around a tree at the bottom of the mountain, about 10 feet wide, and maybe six feet deep. There was a moment of utter silence. The sled caught air as it launched itself into the crater. The *whrrr* noise stopped, and in that one instant, even time seemed to stand still. Then came a muffled *thud* as the machine buried itself in the bottom of the six-foot hole, graveyard style.

Not good. I tried to get up, but a sharp pain shot through my inner right thigh and I yelped and sat down fast. The pain made my eyes water. There was no way I could put even a little bit of weight on that leg. Not good at all.

I lay there in the cold silence wondering what to do next,

but there wasn't much I could do other than wait. I wasn't worried about getting hyperthermia or anything; I knew my buddies would come for me before too long. I was, however, a little worried about my leg. Something was very, very wrong, and I was bleeding.

Sure enough, within a couple minutes I heard the drone of a snowmobile approach and one of my buddies pulled up beside me.

"Gary! What happened?" he asked.

I explained what had happened and said, "I can't put any weight on this leg at all."

"Do you think you can get onto my snowmobile if I help you?" he asked.

I thought about that, "We could try."

Trying was a bad idea. The pain was intense. It was clear that I would not be riding a snowmobile again today.

"Okay, you hang tight, I'm going to go and get more help," my friend said.

"I'm not going anywhere," I said, grimly.

It was impressive how quickly the rescue team from Cooke City got to me. I guess they've done that kind of thing a time or two. What followed next was a claustrophobic's nightmare—good thing I'm not. They lifted me onto a rescue toboggan and strapped me in like an Eskimo baby. I couldn't move a finger. They towed me down the mountain behind a snowmobile. It was weird being so helpless and incapable of motion, but the ride down the hill was nowhere near as weird as getting shoved into the tail of the rescue helicopter that was to fly me to the hospital in Billings. I felt like a missile being loaded into the barrel of a great big gun. Any moment someone could push a button and I'd go shooting off.

There was a paramedic sitting closer to me than my prom date ever did. She asked, "Do you want morphine, Gary?"

Do you ask that of all your dates? "No, thank you just the same. I'd rather know how bad things are hurting," I replied.

"Okay, but let me know if you change your mind," she replied, and turned her attention to a mess of instruments that were a mere 10 inches from my face.

The flight took about 40 minutes. We landed at the St. Vincent Healthcare hospital in Billings. They ejected me like a spent cartridge and got me into an operating room.

There was an anesthesiologist standing to my left, holding a syringe big enough to inseminate a cow. A doctor was to my right, inspecting my leg. He poked around a little and then said to the anesthesiologist, "He's going to need two of those."

Great.

The upshot of all this was that I crushed my femoral artery. Now, my blood had to find a new way of getting to my toes. It would take six weeks for the wound to stop oozing, and even longer for my blood to find new routes. I think "unpleasant" wouldn't be overstating it. I spent the night at the hospital and the next day when the doctor came to see me, I said, "So Doc, can I go?"

"I don't think so, Gary. You know I decided not to close the wound. I want it to be able to drain, but when doing that, it's more vulnerable to infection. I think you should stay another day."

I looked around the room and said, "Uh, don't you think a hospital is the worst place for me to be if you're worried about infection? I mean, every germ in the state makes a pilgrimage here."

He laughed and said, "You'll be fine if you just keep the dressing on it."

"Well, I can keep the dressing on it just fine from the comfort of the Skyline Guest Ranch," I knew I had him there, and he knew it too.

"I suppose . . ." he said reluctantly. "You need to change the dressing regularly and keep it very clean."

I nodded, "Yeah, I can do that."

"And one last thing," he said.

"What?"

"You have to promise me to stay off your snowmobile until you've had a chance to heal."

"No problem," I lied.

My nephew Jeff picked me up. We made a quick stop to buy a pair of crutches, and then back to the parking lot. I was surprised how well my sled had survived the ordeal. The 10-mile ride back to the ranch went pretty easily thanks to some good pain pills. Thanks doc!

● ● ● ●

39 • TENDING THE BUCKET LIST

BUCKET LIST:
1. ~~Marry a wonderful woman~~
2. ~~Raise good kids~~
3. ~~Have good friends~~
4. ~~Have good career~~
5. Ride a motorcycle with Ginny to Alaska

In 2008, Ginny and I decided it was time to cross off an item that had been on our mutual bucket list for a long time. We rode a motorcycle to Alaska.

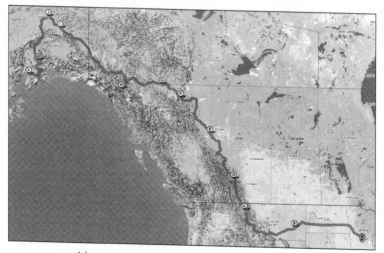

Motorcycle route from Minnesota to Alaska.

We took my BMW K1200LT touring bike. We weren't going to be doing any off-road adventures with it, but on the highways, it rode like a passenger train: first class all the way. Ginny had a nice, high seat behind me and, given the hours we'd spend in the saddle, we were both very comfortable on the bike.

We packed the two panniers and the trunk with clothes, then added a two-man backpack tent and a watertight bag with one sleeping bag (we made that work in the Boundary Waters Canoe Area years ago, so we figured we could do it again). The tent was just in case we couldn't find a hotel at any point. We weren't planning on roughing it, we just wanted to see all there was to see.

Our spirits were high when we pulled out of the driveway in Minnesota, and they stayed that way for the rest of that wonderfully memorable trip. We drove through South Dakota into Montana, where we stopped to visit our snowmobile friends. To relieve the tension that built up with long hours in the saddle, Ginny would pound on my back to the beat of music we both liked. She's a good travel companion.

We made our way into British Columbia, Canada. We travelled through the middle of that magnificent province visiting Lake Louise, Banff, and Jasper—all stunning places, with a postcard photo every mile—until we finally got to the starting point of the Alaska Highway, a.k.a. the Alcan Highway, at Dawson Creek.

Ever since Alaska became a state, the United States wanted road access through B.C., but they could never come to an agreement. It was the Japanese threat to the west coast and Aleutian Islands that finally got the job done in 1942. The U.S. built it and then turned it over to Canada after the war. Canada maintains it and rebuilds it when necessary. From its starting point in B.C., the Alaska Highway runs 1,390 miles northwest and officially ends in Alaska, 95 miles from Fairbanks. They finished paving it in 1981, but even today it's difficult to predict what kind of condition it will be in due to extremes of climate causing potholes, gravel breaks, deteriorated shoulders, bumps, and frost heaves. In other words, we loved it.

It was common to see deer, elk, bears, bison, and sometimes even mountain sheep along the sides of the road. We generally met friendly people and had good accommodations, but there were notable exceptions. One such stop was a widening of the road called Toad River. We were good and ready to get out of the saddle, get some food down us, and have a good night's sleep. There was only one small motel in "town" that was a combo motel/restaurant/bus station/gas station. Having dismounted the bike and given my back a good stretch, I walked toward the motel office where an older lady with black hair and gray roots was standing just outside the door, smoking a cigarette.

"Hi there," I said.

She looked at me, took a deep drag from the cigarette before dropping it and crushing it under her shoe. She blew out the smoke and said, "Evenin'. I guess you want a room?" and we walked into the office.

"Yes, please," I said.

"Well, all I've got left is a room with two singles. It's $75 bucks a night," she looked at me expectantly.

"Guess I'll take it then," I said, pulling out my wallet.

"All right," she reached into a drawer for a key and the paperwork. I filled in the particulars, and took the key.

"Have a good night," I said.

"Yup. You too," she said and turned to a T.V. that was tuned to the CBC evening news. She started a coughing fit as I walked out the door.

Ginny and I carried our stuff to the room. When we walked

in, I could barely believe it because we could barely fit! There were two small beds made up with gold and avocado bedspreads, with just enough room for one person to pass in between. A black and white T.V. (*a black and white T.V.?!*) hung precariously from the wall. Had it fallen, it would have landed on a floor that smelled vaguely of dirty mop. The shower was a narrow stall with just enough room to turn around in, and the toilet ran. Still, it was a dry place to put our heads down for the night. It was bigger than the tent, and there were no bear threats. We were golden.

Not ready for sleep and not wanting to stay in the room, I decided to head down to the restaurant. Ginny opted to stay behind with a book. I seated myself close to the window, so I could watch motorists pass by. A well-fed waitress approached my table with a bit of a scowl. I smiled at her and she stretched her lips back at me.

"What'll you have?" she asked.

"Decaf coffee please," I said.

Then, she looked at me like I'd said something truly offensive and replied, "We don't recognize decaf coffee here."

I blinked at her. That was the weirdest thing I'd heard in days. "Okay, I'll have regular coffee then. Black."

The next morning, we left in a light rain. Mist hung low on the mountains and the landscape had a soft, gentle quality. The road, however, did not. I hit a puddle which was, in fact, more like a small crater, like the Mariana Trench. I hit so hard that both of my breakaway mirrors broke away and flew off, bounced onto the pavement, and slid along for many, many feet. Ginny was clinging to me like a cold sweat as I pulled over as quickly as I could. First, I checked to see that I still had a wife aboard.

"You okay?" I asked.

Ginny pulled off her helmet and blinked, "Yes, I think so.

A little shaken. You'd better go and get those mirrors before a truck runs over them."

The mirrors were much worse for the wear, but I was still able to snap them back on, however, there was a good crack in one. Still, considering that we hit the puddle hard enough to knock off the mirrors and rattle my teeth, I considered us lucky. That could have gone much worse. Ginny had climbed off the bike and was stretching.

"You sure you're okay?" I asked again.

"Oh yes, I'm a tough nut to crack," she smiled.

A tough nut indeed. Ginny has spent the better part of her lifetime traveling to various developing countries and teaching the Word of God. She's been to Isreal at least 20 times. The woman is a force to be reconed with.

Soon, we rolled into Liard Springs, B.C., an area known for its natural hot springs. We decided to go for a nice, long soak. Trees and ferns surrounded the pool, and there was a wooden building where we could change into our bathing suits. There were stairs leading down into the pool, which was large—almost like a big creek. The pool had an upper and lower part, partitioned by a low dam with two "spillways." We could sit in the lower pool, under the spillway in about three feet of falling water. It was bliss to have the hot water pound all the tension out of our bodies, especially after so many days on the bike. What a gem.

The rest of the ride was amazing. Sharp mountains pierced soft clouds. Lazy rivers meandered through low valleys, or roared down sheer cliffs in a spray, leaving rainbows in their wake. The freshness of the air cleared every cell of my body of any toxin or weight, leaving me energized and full of health. Practically every turn brought something new to gape at.

When we reached the official end of the highway in Delta Junction, Alaska, we bought certificates that read, "I survived the Alcan Highway." I'm sure I still have them tucked away somewhere. It was amusing, but I also remember thinking that we didn't merely survive it, we *thrived* it!

The rear tire of the bike, however, was not thriving by the time we hit Delta Junction. The nearest BMW dealer was in Fairbanks, 95 miles away. I drove, or rather, nursed the bike for the next hour and a half with threads showing on the bald tire. It was with high hopes tinged with trepidation that we limped into the dealership; would they have what we needed, or would we have to wait a week for parts? Lady luck was with us, and we were out the door two hours later with a brand-new tire. Next stop, Anchorage.

On the 4th of July, we celebrated Independence Day with our friends Chris and Marsha Ball who lived in Anchorage. Chris and I made an evening run down to the Russian River to fish for what locals affectionately referred to as "Russian reds." Sockeye salmon, as they're more commonly known, are the fightingest fish, pound-for-pound, that I've ever tied into. As fun as they are on the line, they are equally delicious on the grill. Fishing in the dark on a stream in the middle of the Kenai Peninsula wilderness has its risks; it's wise to carry a sidearm. However, a flashlight was not necessary as it was a bright evening with a fullish moon and some northern lights. Besides, after a lifetime of fishing, I can tie a fly onto a line while blindfolded.

Having taken our time coming north, and not wanting to rush our southern trip home, we decided to store the bike for the winter, fly home, and fly back again to pick up where we left off the next summer. We drove 50 miles north of Anchorage to Wasilla and left the BMW at the Denali Harley Davidson shop. For the rest of the winter I looked forward to our trip back again.

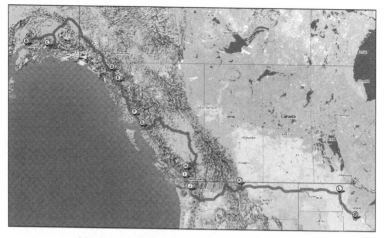

Motorcycle route from Alaska to Minnesota.

When we returned the next summer, it was with great affection for the BMW and anticipation for the adventures to come that I cleaned the dust off the bike and loaded up the panniers and trunk. Ginny was all smiles as she pulled on her helmet for the first time that year.

When we were ready to go, we headed south down the Richardson Highway to Valdez, and continued south to Haines. Just before we arrived in town, we pulled over to ogle the most amazing event. There were hundreds, literally hundreds, of bald eagles on a riverbank. Why they were there, I couldn't be sure. Maybe there were fish spawning and the birds were feeding on the roe and other fish that feed on roe, or maybe it was a breeding ground, I don't know, but the site was spectacular. One tree alone must have had 20 eagles in it!

From Haines, we bought a berth on a ferry and headed to Juneau. From there, we rode to the Mendenhall glacier. I had been there 10 years before and was excited to show Ginny. Although the glacier was still very impressive, it was shocking to see how much it had receded in just one decade. We only had a day in Juneau. The next day the ferry took us to Ketchikan. There, we had even less time, two hours, but we had enough time to stroll through town and enjoy a wonderful dinner before ferrying along to Prince Rupert, B.C.

After disembarking in Prince Rupert, we followed roads flanked by snow-capped mountains and chalky-green rivers all the way to Vancouver where we stayed overnight and took in some of the spectacular gardens. It was strange getting back into so much population again after the solitude and vastness of Alaska and northern BC.

From Vancouver, we crossed into the States and had a quick visit with a cousin of mine who lives in Everett. From there we made our way home through the northern states. By the time we got home, I was truly ready for a good, hot bath, and a long sleep. As great as the trip had been, it's always good to get back home again, too.

● ● ● ●

40 • FUN AND GAMES WITH RUBY

I DECIDED THAT AFTER SO many years of fishing and hunting, there was really no need to prove anything to anyone, not even myself. So, on a hunting trip to Colorado, I knew that hiking up to my elk blind, a two-mile climb of over 600 feet, would certainly put my cardiovascular system into a high-speed wobble. Common sense prevailed, and I chose to rent a horse.

A wrangler delivered a light-brown mare to me the afternoon before the hunt. I ran my hand down her neck, along her side, and over her rump. She seemed sturdy enough.

"What's her name?" I asked the wrangler.

He spat some brown chewing tobacco into the grass, true cowboy style, and said, "3634." I wasn't surprised to hear it, since it was branded on her rump.

"Not much of a name," I said.

"Nope. I guess you can call 'er whatever you want," then he looked at me sideways and squinted from under the brim of his hat and added, "But don't go calling her 'Bucky' or 'Buckaroo' or somethin' stupid like that."

I laughed and said, "Don't worry. I'll figure something out." The wrangler just grunted and tucked another pinch of tobacco under his lip. I don't think he was overly concerned. Soon, he got in his truck and rattled down the road.

Hungry, I rummaged around my pack and came up with a candy bar. The plastic wrapper I tucked back into the bag read

"Babe Ruth." I wandered over to horse 3634, scratched her behind the ears, looked into her big dark eyes, and asked, "How would you like to be called *Ruby?*"

She half closed her eyes as I scratched, and she seemed perfectly contented to be called *Late for Dinner*, just as long as I kept on scratching her like that.

"Ruby it is," I declared, pleased. I decided to take her for an introduction ride, so I saddled her up, and we rode over some hills and crossed a few streams. I was good to her. She was good to me. It was a good start. We returned to camp where I removed her saddle and let her graze for the evening.

The next morning was a Saturday. At 4:00 a.m., well before sunup, I saddled Ruby, threw some provisions into a small bag, and put my 300 Weatherby Magnum rifle into my Kolpin scabbard. We were off for our first day of hunting.

Ruby seemed to be good with crossing water. Some horses aren't, and they'll stop dead before crossing. They'd rather get their hides smacked than get their feet wet, but Ruby wasn't like that. She was fine the night before and this morning, in the dark, she didn't have any troubles crossing the first creek. The second creek was a different story.

I don't know if it was the water she didn't like, or the brush on the other side of the creek that caught her attention, but I do know that once we were in the water, she took off suddenly, and jumped straight up the bank. I lost my seat and landed on a small piece of flat ground, luckily devoid of logs or rocks. Still, I landed flat on my chest and had the wind knocked out of me. When I finally caught my breath and got mobile again, Ruby was nowhere.

Horses . . .

I listened hard for any sounds of a large animal making her way through trees and bush, but it was as silent as it was dark. Sunrise was still more than two hours away.

I wonder if she'd make her way back to camp like a dog would? I thought to myself, so I hiked back from where we came, but there was no Ruby. In the dark, I searched the creek bottom for an hour before giving up and sitting down on a deadfall. I poured myself a cup of Joe from the thermos I found after getting thrown and thought about it some more. *Where would she go? Does she still have my rifle? Can I shoot her with it when I find her?*

I decided that at first light, I would return to the scene where she'd bucked me off and then take the path of least resistance. This turned out to be a gentle uphill walk through a sparse stand of aspens. In about a quarter of a mile, I found her standing there; just standing there and staring at me with absolutely no expression. Her saddle had loosened. It was hanging, along with my scabbard and rifle, under her belly.

"Hello, Ruby," I cooed as I slowly approached her, not wanting her to spook.

"Hello, Gary," she said, "It would be lovely if you would be so kind as to sort this mess out. I seem to have gotten myself all tangled up."

"Looks like you've got yourself all tangled up," I said.

"Yes," she replied, "That's what I just said."

I undid the saddle and rearranged the gear, then mounted and rode her up the mountain. We finally got to the hunting spot about two hours too late. There would be no elk this morning.

Ruby: 1, Gary: 0

On day two, I saddled Ruby up at 4:00 a.m. again, and we set off as we had the day before. This time I was very careful about crossing the creeks, and there were no more incidents with them. However, I learned something about horses that I never knew before. Apparently, horses like to run uphill. I had noticed a rule in the paperwork when I was renting her that indicated riders were not supposed to run the horses uphill. It seemed like an odd thing to put into the rules, but at the time I figured they'd had some incident at some point with an idiot and they were just being reactive by putting it into the rules for everyone, but as it turns out, it's a "thing." Horses like to run uphill.

Sure enough, as Ruby and I began to climb a particularly steep part of the mountain, she started to run. I tried to rein her back and she jerked her head up and then started to come over backward. I tried to bail off to the side, so she didn't land on me, but I couldn't get clear of her in time. She rolled over my legs and groin.

She kept on rolling and the moment she cleared off me, I did a quick scan of my limbs and hips and found everything working. By now, Ruby had stopped rolling and was on her back with all four of her legs flailing around in the air. She looked like a big, overturned beetle. Then she twisted sideways and got her hind legs wrapped around an eight-inch aspen tree. We were still on loose ground and her legs were still all twisted up, when the rest of her started sliding down the hill again. She spun around the tree and ended up smacking her head against the hard ground with a *thud* that I heard *and* felt. She went limp.

Is she dead? Was my first thought. I got up and checked her out. She seemed to still be breathing. She had knocked herself out cold. *Now what?* I had the thought that I might have to shoot her if she had broken a leg or two. At that point, it seemed like maybe not a bad idea. At least she'd gotten me a few hundred yards further than she had the morning before.

After about five minutes, I unsaddled her, and I decided that I'd better get her tied up in case she came-to and opted to bolt. The moment I tugged on her halter rope, she came to life in a big way. She struggled to untangle herself and find her feet again. I kept clear as she thrashed and eventually managed to stand. Once she was up, I walked her around and found that she had a slight limp in her hind leg but otherwise seemed okay.

"Alright you," I told her sternly, "I've had about enough of your shenanigans."

Ruby snorted, "Shenanigans? You make it sound like I did that on purpose! Personally, I'd rather you just leave me right here for the day. Who needs to be running up and down mountains?"

I told her, "I'm going to leave you right here for the day."

She blinked.

I tied to her to a tree with enough rope for her to graze, and set off on foot in the dark, crisp, thin mountain air. I found no elk that day, but at least I didn't miss them on account of a silly horse.

Ruby:0, Gary:1

When I returned to Ruby, about an hour before sunset, she seemed happy to see me—maybe even a little sheepish. I was concerned about her leg, so I saddled her up and then led her back down the mountain and across the two small creeks. She managed that okay, so I rode her the last 300 yards into camp.

I'd dodged two bullets now, and two is a pattern. Given that the only trouble Ruby'd given me had always been in the dark, I decided to only ride her in daylight. That seemed to work because the next four days were event-free. Still, I was only too happy to hand her over to the tobacco-spitting wrangler at the end of the week. Ruby returned to being horse #3634, and I returned to being a two-legged hunter.

I may very well die on the side of a mountain someday, but it won't be because of a horse.

41 ● PERSONAL BEST

IN 2013, PRECO SOLD SPECTRALYTICS to another company called Cretex. At that point, I transitioned into a consultant role and no longer did the day-to-day running and decision making. Like a child, a business—no matter how much you love it—has to be let go of at some point, and that point had come. Although it was a big change, retirement, it was very good for my golf game. I got to spend more time with Ginny, and of course I spent a lot more time fishing and hunting too. Some guys don't handle retirement well, especially when they've invested most of their intellectual and emotional energy into their work, but I did okay. I attribute that to the fact that I've always had a well-rounded life, so the loss of work wasn't the loss of everything.

By 2017, I'd been hunting deer for 62 years. I'd been all over my home turf, travelled to the wilds of Canada, and scoured the primordial woods of Alaska in search of game. I've learned a few things along the way, made a few mistakes, caught a few wins; but the biggest win I ever caught came to me in the early afternoon on a sunny November day, just a short drive from my own home.

I'd been hunting near Rose City for three days, based out of a cabin owned by my friend Jeff and my brother, Don. It was Saturday, the last weekend of a nine-day season, and a fine day for a walk in the woods. I carried a Benneli shotgun with a

271

Leopold scope that I'd loaded with 300-grain SPX Winchester sabot slugs—I was ready. I'd seen a fair amount of game since I'd been out, but I'd passed on everything because it was too small. However, the season was coming quickly to a close, so I decided it was time to take a small buck or a doe that was not with fawns. I wanted something for the freezer and to contribute to the Cornerstone Game Feed.

Even though it was still early in the afternoon, I settled into my deer stand and waited. I hadn't even had time to get impatient when just such a doe came by. She was picking her way through some tall grass and brush, which was frustrating because she gave me no clear shot. As it turned out, this was a good thing. Not 20 yards behind her, I spotted a tall set of tines moving through the tall weeds with sunlight bouncing off them. Then I could see the massive neck and shoulders of a magnificent buck—and I do mean magnificent.

He was hot on the trail of the doe in heat and had only one thing on his mind. This was good news for me because when he paused to get a whiff of the doe, I had my chance. I knew I would only get one shot at this, so I put my duplex cross hairs on his lungs, took a quick breath, held it, and squeezed the trigger. The slug exited the barrel at 1,850 feet per second, entered the animal's boiler room, and he dropped like an auctioneer's gavel.

I could barely believe what I saw lying there in the tall grass that day. He was a 14-point buck with a drop tine. The drop tine is rare in our area, so I was particularly pleased to see that. He would later weigh in at 198 pounds. His unofficial Boone & Crockett net-score was 157 5/8. A personal best. Officially, I was one happy hunter!

I field dressed the buck but there was no way I could drag him out of the woods. I had to leave him for a few minutes while I went back for my Jeep. Fortunately, I was able to drive right up to him. (Okay, I did have to bowl over a few small trees, and I ended up with a pile of branches on the hood.) With a mighty effort and the use of some strategically placed ratchet straps, I was able to load the behemoth onto the Jeep, one end at a time. The drive back to the log cabin with my trophy kind of felt like doing a victory lap. What a win!

Note to self: sometimes the best things in life are right here at home.

• • • •

Me and my beautiful wife Ginny.

42 ● REFLECTION

LATER, AS I SAT AT home on the first day of 2018, smelling the tantalizing odors that Ginny was creating in the kitchen, I got to thinking about sidetracks. Very early on in life, way back on the farm, I realized that I wasn't going to get what I wanted out of life by following the crowd. No, I would need to forge my own way.

I looked up at my 57-inch moose rack from Alaska, my newly aquired whitetail deer rack, a half of an antler that reminds me to keep my gun close by, a beautiful mounted arctic grayling that I caught in Saskatchewan, and a slew of framed photos of my children and friends and family, and finally, a nearby Bible. I felt an overwhelming and profound sense of fullness and gratitude.

I thought of *The Lone Cowboy* and of how I used to pour over Herter's catalogs. I remembered all the teachings from my mom and dad and uncles and aunts and how they shaped the man I was to become. I remembered the moment I laid eyes on my Ginny, and how fine she looked that night. I remember the look on her face when she first handed me each of my newborn babies. I remembered so many of my adventures with Quint, the years at the Chute, and I remembered his funeral. How worried I was about Dawn when I met with her boyfriend's father, who would become one of my best friends. I thought of the decades I've been going to the Lake of the Woods and all the good times we've had there. How many times have I been to Alaska? How many fish have I caught in my lifetime? How many campfires have I built? The mountains and forests, lakes and rivers are all a part of me now; they're my bones and muscles, my arteries and veins. I reflected on my career, rich with experiences and accomplishments. I thought of all the good times, all the good friends, and all the wonderful family that I am so deeply blessed with. I'm not given to emotion, but in that moment, I felt so overwhelmed with joy and gratitude for all the blessings that God has bestowed on me that I felt I would nearly burst with it all.

Then, in the quiet, I heard my old friend Quint's voice echoing off the walls.

"You know Gary, you should write a book."

* * * *

ABOUT THE AUTHOR

GARY OBERG has spent his life on the edge. As an engineer and entrepreneur, he's taken a lot of chances, but he really learned about risk mitigation over a lifetime of pushing the limits outdoors. He grew up on a farm in 1950s Minnesota, where he learned to appreciate nature and her ways, and spent much of his life fishing and hunting throughout North America. These are the stories he's accumulated over 70 years, and the lessons they've taught him. Told with much humor and humility, his tales are a celebration of God's creations, comedic failures, and gratifying triumphs. From duck-hunting in the marshes of Minnesota, to fishing the pristine lakes of Ontario, to bagging moose in the jagged peaks of Alaska, Gary writes about all the compelling characters, all the blessings, and all the curses of living life on the edge—where, "if you're not living on the edge, you're takin' up too much room."